The Resurrection and the Hereafter

from the Risale-i Nur Collection
Humanity's Encounter with the Divine Series

The Resurrection and the Hereafter

- *The Resurrection and the Hereafter (10th Word)*
- *Answers to Questions about Paradise (28th Word)*
- *Doomsday and the Afterlife (29th Word)*

Bediüzzaman
SAİD NURSİ

New Jersey

Copyright © 2022 by Tughra Books
First Published 2002
25 24 23 22   4 5 6 7

Published by Tughra Books
335 Clifton Ave.
Clifton, NJ, 07011, USA

www.tughrabooks.com

Translated from Turkish by Ali Ünal

Library of Congress Cataloging-in-Publication Data
Nursi, Said, 1877-1960.
The resurrection and the hereafter / Bediuzzaman Said Nursi. p. cm.
-- (Humanity's encounter with the divine ; 2)
"From the Risale-i Nur collection."
Includes index.
ISBN 0-9720654-0-7 (pbk.)
     1.Eschatology, Islamic. 2. Resurrection (Islam) 3. Future life-
    - Islam. 4. Islam--Doctrines. 5. Nurculuk I. Title. II. Series.
    BP166.8.N87 2002 297.2'3--dc21

                     2002006831

ISBN: 978-0-9720654-0-5

Table of Contents

Bediüzzaman and the Risale-i Nur

In the many dimensions of his lifetime of achievement, as well as in his personality and character, Bediüzzaman (1877-1960) was and, through his continuing influence, still is an important thinker and writer in the Muslim world. He represented in a most effective and profound way the intellectual, moral and spiritual strengths of Islam, evident in different degrees throughout its fourteen-century history. He lived for eighty-five years. He spent almost all of those years, overflowing with love and ardor for the cause of Islam, in a wise and measured activism based on sound reasoning and in the shade of the Qur'an and the Prophetic example.

Bediüzzaman lived in an age when materialism was at its peak and many crazed after communism, and the world was in great crisis. In that critical period, Bediüzzaman pointed people to the source of belief and inculcated in them a strong hope for a collective restoration. At a time when science and philosophy were used to mislead young generations into atheism, and nihilistic attitudes had a wide appeal, at a time when all this was done in the name of civilization, modernization and contemporary thinking and those who tried to resist them were subjected to the cruelest of persecutions, Bediüzzaman strove for the overall revival of a whole people, breathing into their minds whatever and spirits whatever is taught in the institutions of both modern and traditional education and of spiritual training.

Bediüzzaman had seen that modern unbelief originated from science and philosophy, not from ignorance as previously. He wrote that nature is the collection of Divine signs and therefore science and religion cannot be conflicting disciplines. Rather, they are two (apparently) different expressions of the same truth. Minds should be enlightened with sciences, while hearts need to be illumined by religion.

Bediüzzaman was not a writer in the usual sense of the word. He wrote his splendid work the *Risale-i Nur*, a collection exceeding 5,000 pages, because he had a mission: he struggled against the materialistic and atheistic trends of thought fed by science and philosophy and tried to present the truths of Islam to modern minds and hearts of every level of understanding. The *Risale-i Nur*, a modern commentary of the Qur'an, mainly concentrates on the existence and unity of God, the Resurrection, Prophethood, the Divine Scriptures primarily including the Qur'an, the invisible realms of existence, Divine Destiny and humanity's free will, worship, justice in human life, and humanity's place and duty among the creation.

In order to remove from people's minds and hearts the accumulated 'sediment' of false beliefs and conceptions and to purify them both intellectually and spiritually, Bediüzzaman writes forcefully and makes reiterations. He writes in neither an academic nor a didactic way; rather he appeals to feelings and aims to pour out his thoughts and ideas into people's hearts and minds in order to awaken them to belief and conviction.

This book includes selected sections from the *Risale-i Nur* collection.

The Resurrection and the Hereafter

[Note: I use metaphors and parables to ease compre-hension and show how rational, proper, consistent, and coherent are the truths of Islam. The inner mean-ings are contained in the truths concluding them. Each story is like an allusion pointing to these truths. So, in this sense, they are not fictions but, rather, undoubted truths.]

In the Name of God,
the Merciful, the Compassionate.

Look upon the signs and imprints of God's Mercy, how He revives Earth after its death. He it is Who will revive the dead [in the same way]. He is pow-erful over all things. (30:50)

If you wish to hear about the Resurrection and the Hereafter in simple language and style, listen to this parable: Two people[1] went to a Paradise-

---

[1] God declares in the Qur'an: *I shall not allow to go to waste the deed of any one of you, whether male or female. You are one from the other* (3:195). It is clear that Islam does not discriminate between men and women in religious

like land (this world). They saw all doors opened and shops unlocked, as if the people did not care about protecting their possessions. The first one took whatever he wanted and, following his desire, committed every kind of injustice and indecency. The people did almost nothing to stop him.

His friend asked: "What are you doing? You'll be punished, and you'll get me into trouble too! This property is collectively owned, for these people are soldiers or government servants. They're working as civilians now, and so aren't interfering so much with you. But the order is strict. The king has installed phones, and his officers are everywhere. Go and seek forgiveness!" The foolish, obstinate man replied: "No, this property

_____

responsibility. Each gender shares most of the responsibilities, but each one has certain responsibilities that are particular to it. The Qur'an usually uses the masculine form of address, for this is one of Arabic's characteristics. In almost every language, the masculine form is used for a group comprising both men and women, like the English word *mankind*, which includes both men and women. So, *brotherhood* also includes sisterhood, and, since the believers comprise both male and female believers, the believers are brothers and sisters. However, in order to maintain the original text and avoid repetition, usually we do not mention the feminine forms in translation. (Tr.)

belongs to some charity or other and has no owner. Everyone can use it as he or she pleases. Why shouldn't I use these fine things? I won't believe unless I see with my own eyes." He also spoke, as might a philosopher, a lot of sophistry.

A debate ensued. When the obstinate one asked: "Who is the king? I don't know him," his friend said: "Every village must have a headman, every needle a manufacturer and craftsperson, and every letter a writer. How could such an extremely well-ordered land have no ruler? How could such wealth have no owner, when a train filled with precious and artful gifts arrives hourly, as if coming from the Realm of the Unseen?[2] It unloads here and goes on. Every announcement and proclamation, each seal and stamp found on those goods, all coins and flags waving throughout the kingdom—how could they have no owner? It seems you have acquired some training in a foreign culture, for you can read the foreign, but not the Islamic, script. You also refuse to ask those who can read it. Come now, let me read the supreme decree to you."

---

[2] The train indicates a year, as each spring is a carload of provisions coming from the Unseen.

The obstinate one retorted: "Even if there is a king, I'm using so little of his wealth that he can't possibly be hurt by this. What will it diminish in his treasury? I see no prison here, so why should I worry about being punished?" His friend replied: "Be serious! This land is a maneuvering ground, an exhibition of the king's wonderful royal arts, a temporary hospice. Can't you see that a caravan arrives daily as another one departs and vanishes? It's constantly filled and emptied. Soon the land will be changed. Its people will be transported to another, and eternal, land where they will be rewarded or punished for their service."

That unbeliever stated: "I don't believe it. How can this land perish and move to another place?" His faithful friend answered: "Let me show you, O obstinate and rebellious one, some of the innumerable proofs that what I've told you is true."

Twelve pictures

FIRST PICTURE: Could such a magnificent kingdom not have a system of reward for those who obey and of punishment for those who rebel? As reward and punishment are virtually non-existent here, there must be a Supreme Tribunal somewhere else.

SECOND PICTURE: Look at this organization and administration. Everyone, including the poorest and the weakest, receives the most appropriate and perfect sustenance. The lonely and sick receive the best care. Notice the royal and delicious foods, dishes, jeweled decorations, embroidered clothes, magnificent feasts. Everyone takes their duties seriously, except for rebels like you, and do not transgress their bounds. The greatest people are engaged in modest and obedient service, and work in an attitude of fear and awe.

Given this, the ruler must have great generosity and an all-embracing compassion, great dignity, and the most exalted honor and high state. Generosity requires liberality, compassion cannot be dispensed without beneficence, and honor and high state require that the discourteous be chastised. But not even a minute part of what that compassion and high state require is visible here. The oppressor remains powerful and the oppressed humiliated. As they both depart and migrate from this realm, their affairs must be left to a Supreme Tribunal.

THIRD PICTURE: All affairs are managed with lofty wisdom and order; transactions are effected with true justice and balance. A wise polity requires that seekers of the state's protecting wing receive favor. Justice demands that subjects' rights be preserved so that the government's dignity and the state's authority and splendor are maintained. But only a minute part of that is fulfilled here. Disobedient people like you often leave this realm unpunished. Their affairs must be left to a Supreme Tribunal.

FOURTH PICTURE: Look at the innumerable and peerless jewels displayed like great dishes at a banquet. The ruler must have an inexhaustible treasury and infinite generosity, both of which deserve and require a bountiful and eternal display of all objects of desire as well as the eternal nature of those enjoying the feast, so that they will not suffer pain due to death or separation until eternity. Just as pain's end brings pleasure, pleasure's end brings pain.

Look at these displays and listen to the announcements. Heralds proclaim the miracle-working monarch's fine and delicate arts. They show his perfections, declare his matchless and invisible beauty, and tell of his hidden beauty's subtle manifestations. Given this, he must have an amazing beauty and perfection that is not seen here. This hidden perfection requires one who will appreciate and admire it, who will gaze on it and exclaim: "What wonders God has willed!" thus displaying it and making it known.

Concealed and matchless beauty wills to see and be seen, to contemplate itself in mirrors and via the contemplations of ecstatic spectators and amazed admirers. It wills to see and be seen, to contemplate itself eternally, and to be contemplated without cease. It wills permanent existence for those who gaze upon it in awe and joy, for eternal beauty cannot be content with transient admirers.

Moreover, admirers destined to perish without hope of return will find their love changed into enmity whenever they imagine their death. Such admiration and respect will lean toward contempt, for we are enemies of what we do not know and cannot reach. However, we leave this guest-house quickly and vanish, after having seen, for only a moment, a dim light or shadow of that perfection and beauty. As this sight does not satisfy us, we know that we are moving toward an eternal realm of seeing.

FIFTH PICTURE: Given the above, that peerless being also has infinite mercy. He quickly sends aid to every afflicted or unfortunate one. He answers every request and petition, even the lowliest subject's lowliest need. If, for example, the foot of a herdsman's sheep should hurt, he provides medicine or sends a veterinarian.

Come on, let's go to a great meeting being held in that land. All nobles of the land have assembled there. A most noble commander, one bearing an exalted decoration, is petitioning the compassionate king for certain things. Everyone is saying after him: "Yes, yes, we ask for the same." They agree with and affirm his words. Now, listen to what that noble commander, who is best loved by the king, is saying:

> Our Master, you who nurture us with your bounty, show us the origin and true form of these examples and shadows you have shown us. Draw us close to your seat of rule. Don't let us perish in these deserts, but rather admit us to your presence. Have mercy on us. Feed us there on the true form of the exquisite bounty you have caused us to taste here. Don't afflict

us with despair and banishment, or leave your yearning, thankful, and obedient subjects to their own
devices. Don't cause us to be annihilated.

Having heard what he says, could such a merciful and powerful king deny the request of his
most beloved and noble commander's finest and
highest aim? Remember that he fulfills his lowliest soldier's lowliest desire. The commander and
humanity have the same purpose. Moreover, its ful-
fillment is required by the king's pleasure, compassion, and justice.

Such matters are as easy for him as creating
these transient places of enjoyment. Having spent
so much on this transient place, which lasts only
5 or 6 days, to show instances of his power and
benevolence, he will display at his seat of rule true
treasures, perfections, and skills in such a manner, and open before us such spectacles, that our
intellects will be astonished. Those sent to this field
of trial will not be left to their own devices; rather,
palaces of bliss or dungeons of punishment await
them.

SIXTH PICTURE: Come now, look! All these
imposing trains, planes, machines, warehouses, and
exhibitions show that a majestic king exists and

governs behind a veil.[3] Such a sovereign requires subjects worthy of himself. But his subjects are gathered in a guesthouse that is filled and emp-

---

[3] When an army is told to "take up your weapons and fix your bayonets," according to the rules of war while on maneuver, it resembles a forest of oaks. When a garrison's soldiers are commanded on a festive day to wear their parade uniforms and medals, the army resembles an ornate garden full of flowers of every color. This is how it is with all of Earth's species of unfeeling plants and trees that, like animals, jinn, humanity, and animals, are only one of the infinitely various armies of the Eternal King, when they receive the order *Be! And it is* in the struggle for life's maintenance, and the command "Take up your weapons and equipment to defend yourselves and maintain your lives!" At that time, all those plants and trees fix their bayonets, in the form of trees and plants with thorns, and resemble a splendid army standing on the parade or battle ground.

Each spring day and week is like a festive day for each vegetable species. Each species presents itself to the Eternal King's watching and witnessing gaze, with the jeweled decorations He has bestowed on them, as if on parade to display the precious gifts He has given them. It is as if they were obeying His command to "wear the garments produced by Divine artistry and put on the decorations (flowers and fruit) made by His Creativity." At such a time, the face of Earth represents a garrison on a magnificent parade on a splendid festive day that is brilliant with the soldiers' uniforms and jeweled decorations. Such a purposeful and well-arranged equipment and decoration demonstrates, to all who are not blind, that

tied daily. Moreover, his subjects now are gathered on a testing ground for maneuvers, a ground that is changed hourly. Again, his subjects stay in an exhibition hall for a few minutes to behold examples of his beneficence, priceless products of his miraculous art. But the exhibition alters each moment. Whatever leaves does not return, and whatever comes is destined to go. All of this proves that there are permanent palaces and lasting abodes, as well as gardens and treasuries full of the pure and exalted originals of the samples, beyond what we see here. This is why we exert ourselves here. We work here, and he rewards us there with a form and degree of happiness suited to our capacity.

SEVENTH PICTURE: Let's walk and see what is going on. Everywhere you see photographers taking pictures and scribes recording everything, no matter how insignificant or ordinary. The king's supreme photographer, who is devoted to his service and photographs everything, is installed on a tall mountain.[4] The king must have ordered that all

---

they occur only due to the command of a king with infinite power and unlimited wisdom.

[4] Some of these truths are presented in the Seventh Truth: The photographer devoted to the king's service indicates the

transactions and deeds performed in his kingdom be recorded. One day, he will use these records to call his subjects to account.

Would such an All-Wise and All-Preserving Being not record His greatest subject's—humanity's—most significant deeds? Would He not call everyone to account in order to reward or punish them? After all, people do things that offend His glory, are contrary to His pride, and are unacceptable to His compassion. They remain unpunished in this world, and so must be called before a Supreme Tribunal (somewhere else).

EIGHTH PICTURE: Let me read the king's decrees to you. He makes the following promises and threats many times: "I will take you from your present abode and bring you to the realm of

---

Supreme Preserved Tablet. This Tablet's reality and existence is proved in The Twenty-sixth Word as follows: A little portfolio suggests the existence of a great ledger; a little document points to the existence of a great register; and little drops point to the existence of a great water tank. Thus our retentive faculties, a tree's fruits, a fruit's seeds and kernels are like a little portfolio, a miniature guarded tablet, or a drop proceeding from the pen that inscribes the great Guarded Tablet. They all point to, indicate, and prove the existence of a Supreme Memory, a Great Register, an exalted Guarded Tablet.

my absolute rule so that I may bestow happiness on the obedient and imprison the disobedient. I will destroy that temporary abode and establish a different realm containing eternal palaces and dungeons." He does what he promises with great ease, and these promises are very important for his subjects. His dignity and power do not allow him to break his promise.

So reflect, O confused one. Do not listen to your lying imagination, distressed intellect, and deceiving soul, all of which deny the words of one who cannot break his promise, whose high stature allows no deception, and to whose trustworthiness all visible deeds bear witness. You deserve to be punished, for you are like a traveler who closes his eyes to the sunlight in order to follow the light provided by his imagination. You want to illuminate this awesomely dark path with the light of your brain, although it is no more than a glowworm. The king fulfills all his promises, an act that is easy for him and necessary for creation as well as for himself and his kingdom. Thus, there is a Supreme Tribunal and a lofty happiness.

NINTH PICTURE: Look at these office managers and group leaders.[5] Each has a private phone to speak personally with the king. Sometimes they go directly to his presence. All of them say that the king has prepared a magnificent and awesome place for reward and punishment. His promises are emphatic, and his threats are stern. His pride and dignity do not allow him to suffer the humiliation inherent in breaking a promise.

The bearers of this report, who are so numerous as to be universally accepted, unanimously report that the seat and headquarters of the lofty kingdom, some of whose traces are visible here, are located in another realm far from here. The buildings here are temporary and soon will be exchanged for eternal palaces. This world will change, for that magnificent and unfading kingdom, the splendor of which is apparent from its works, cannot be founded or based on something transient, impermanent, unstable, insignificant, changing, defective,

---

[5] Consult the Eight Truth. For example, we use *office managers* and *group leaders* for Prophets and saints, and phone for a link and relation with God that goes forth from the heart, and is Revelation's mirror and inspiration's receptacle. The heart is like the telephone's ear-piece.

and imperfect. It can be based only on matters worthy of it, and which are eternal, stable, permanent, and glorious. Thus there is another realm toward which we are heading.

TENTH PICTURE: Today is the vernal equinox.[6] Certain changes will take place, and wonderful things will happen. On this fine spring day, let's go for a walk on the green plain adorned with beautiful flowers. Other people also are heading for it. Some magic must be at work, for ruins suddenly have become buildings again, and this once-empty plain resembles a populous city. It shows a different scene every hour, just like a movie screen, and assumes a different shape. Note the perfect order among these complex, swiftly changing and numerous scenes, and that each item is put in its prop-

---

[6] These aspects are explained in the Ninth Truth. The equinox represents the beginning of spring, while the green fields full of flowers represent Earth in spring. The changing scenes stand for the creatures, beings, and things in springtime and the provisions given to humanity and animals. These are brought forth in orderly succession, from the beginning of spring to the end of summer, by a Majestic, Powerful Maker, an All-Wise, Gracious Creator, Who renews them with utmost compassion and dispatches them continuously, one after the other.

er place. The imaginary scenes cannot be as well-ordered as this, and millions of skilled magicians could not possess such artistry. Given this, the invisible king must have performed even greater miracles.

O obstinate one! You ask how this vast kingdom can be destroyed and re-established somewhere else. Are you blind to the numerous changes and revolutions that occur hourly, just like the transfer from one realm to another that you deny? This gathering in and scattering forth indicate that a certain purpose is concealed within these visible and swift joinings and separations, these compoundings and dissolvings. It is as if 10 years of effort is devoted to a joining together destined to last no longer than an hour. How can such circumstances be ends in themselves? They are no more than parables indicating or imitating something beyond themselves.

That exalted being brings them about in miraculous fashion, and then they are copied, preserved, and recorded, just as what happens on a battlefield is recorded. This implies that an infinitely vast gathering place will be built, and that what happens therein will be based on what happens here.

Furthermore, the results of what occurs here will be shown permanently at some supreme exposition. All transient and fluctuating phenomena seen here will yield the fruit of eternal and immutable form. Thus all variations observed in this world are for the sake of a supreme happiness, a lofty tribunal, and for exalted aims as yet unknown to us.

ELEVENTH PICTURE: So, my obstinate friend, let's travel through time and see what miraculous works this king has accomplished in other places. We can see similar marvels wherever we go, although they differ with respect to art and form. But the order and harmony betokening manifest wisdom, indications of evident favoring, signs of lofty justice, and fruits of comprehensive mercy still are seen in these transient stations, impermanent spheres, and passing scenes.

Even those with limited insight understand that no one can equal or surpass this king's perfect wisdom, beautiful providence, comprehensive compassion, and glorious justice. If you deny the permanent abodes, lofty places, fixed stations, and permanently resident and contented populations existing in his kingdom—if you deny the full manifestation of the truths of his wisdom, favoring, mercy, and justice in his realm—we would have to deny all that we see in this world.

Could we deny the sun, whose light is clearly visible? Could we consider the source of these wise measures, generous acts, and merciful gifts—all of which are clearly visible—as a trickster or a tyrant? We change truth into its opposite if we answer "yes," although all rational beings say it is impossible. The only exception to this rule are Sophists, for they deny everything. Thus there is another realm that contains a supreme tribunal, a lofty place of justice, and an exalted place of reward. There, all this favoring, wisdom, mercy, and justice will be manifested fully.

TWELFTH PICTURE: Let's visit the chiefs and officers of these groups, check out their equipment, and ask whether it was given so they could survive for a while here or to use it as a means to obtain a life of bliss in another realm. As we cannot do this with everyone, let's look at this officer's identity card and register.

We see that his rank, salary, duty, supplies, and instructions are recorded. His rank is not for just a few days. In fact, it might have been given to him for a prolonged period. It says on his card: "You will receive so much salary on such-and-such a day from the treasury." But the date in question is far in the future, after this realm has been vacated.

Similarly, the duty mentioned on his card is not meant for this temporary realm alone, but rather for the sake of earning permanent happiness via some degree of nearness to the king. His supplies are not meant to ensure his survival here for a few days; they can be only for the sake of a long and happy life. The instructions explain that he is destined for a different place and that he is working for another realm.

Look at these registers. They explain how to use and dispose of these weapons and equipment. If there were no exalted and eternal realm, such a register of categorical instructions and an identity card with clear information would be meaningless. That respected officer, noble commander, and honored chief would be lower than anybody else, for he would be the most wretched, luckless, abased, afflicted, indigent, and weak person. Apply the same principle to everything. Whatever you see testifies to another and eternal world.

This temporary world is like a field, a training ground, a market that will be replaced by a supreme tribunal and ultimate happiness. If you deny this, you must deny all officers' identity cards, equipment, and orders, as well as the country's order, its government, and whatever the government does. If you do so, how can you be considered a true human being or even a conscious being?

The proof for this transfer of creation from one realm to another is not restricted to these Twelve Pictures. Countless other indications and proofs show that this impermanent, changing kingdom will be transferred to a permanent, immutable realm. Innumerable signs and evidences show that we will leave this temporary hospice and be sent to the eternal seat of rule of all creation. I will discuss one proof that is stronger than all Twelve Pictures taken together.

In the midst of the great assembly, the same noble commander we saw earlier is making an announcement. Let's go and listen. He is conveying an imperial edict, hung high over there. He says: "Prepare yourselves. You will go to another and permanent realm, a realm that will make this one seem like a dungeon. You will go to the seat of our king's rule, and receive his compassion and bounty, if you heed and obey this edict. If you rebel and disobey it, you will be cast into awesome dungeons."

Such is the message he conveys. This decree bears a miraculous seal that cannot be imitated. Only obstinate, rebellious people like you do not understand that this is from the king. Moreover, the noble commander bears such bright decorations that everyone, except blind people, understands that he is the truthful conveyor of the king's orders. How can the noble commander be doubted, for doing so would entail denying all that we have seen. So, my friend, what have you got to say for yourself?

My friend replied: "What can I say? What can contradict all of this? Who can speak against the sun at midday? I only can say: 'Praise be to God,' thank Him for saving me from my vain fancy and imagination, and for delivering me from an eternal prison. I believe that there is an abode of happiness in some degree of nearness to the king, one that is separate from this confused and impermanent hospice."

Our parable indicating the truth of the Resurrection and the Hereafter ends here. Now, with God's grace, we will pass on to the most exalted truth. We shall set forth twelve interrelated truths corresponding to the Twelve Pictures discussed above. By means of various indications, we also refer here to several matters also explained elsewhere.[7]

Four indications

FIRST INDICATION: The two people mentioned above correspond to three other pairs:

- The instinct-driven self and the heart [the seat of spiritual intellect].
- Students of philosophy and students of the Wise Qur'an.
- Unbelievers and the community of believers [Muslims].

The worst error and misguidance of each group lies in not recognizing God. As the believer in our parable said: "There can be no letter without a scribe, no law without a legislator." We affirm this.

How can a book, particularly one in whose every word a miniature pen has written another book, and in each letter of which a fine pen has composed a magnificent calligraphic work of praise, lack an author? As this universe is such a book, it must have an Author. Each page includes many books, every

---

[7] In the Nineteenth, Twenty-second, and Twenty-sixth Words.

word a book, and every letter a praise. Earth's surface represents only one page of that Book of the Universe, which comprises innumerable books. Every tree is a word, every fruit a letter, and every seed a dot containing an elaborate tree's index. Such a book could have been inscribed only by the mighty pen of a Majestic One, Who is qualified by the attributes of Majesty and Grace and has infinite Power and Wisdom. Affirming the believer's statement follows necessarily from observing this world, unless one is sunk in delusion.

A house must have an architect, particularly one displaying such astounding artistry, design, and subtle ornament. There is more art in one of its stones than in a whole palace. How could it not have an architect? Its rooms are reshaped and altered hourly, as easily and orderly as changing clothes, or shifting one scene to another on a movie screen. In addition, numerous little rooms are continually created in each scene.

The universe's very existence requires an infinitely wise, all-knowing, and all-powerful maker, for it is a palace whose lamps are the sun and the moon, whose candles are the stars. Within it, time is like a suspended rope upon which the Majestic

Maker threads a new world annually. He renews the world's form or appearance daily with absolute orderliness and wisdom. He makes Earth's surface a bountiful spread that, adorned each spring with countless plant and animal species, is filled with uncountable varieties of generous gifts. Despite their vast abundance, each creature is distinctly individualized and, at the same time, closely related and intermingled. Is it possible to miss the existence of the Maker of such a palace?

How can you deny the sun's existence at noon on a cloudless day, when its presence is reflected in all transparent objects? To do so means you believe that each transparent object contains a miniature, real, and existent sun; that each minute particle contains a massive sun, although that particle has room enough only for itself. How can you logically deny the perfect Attributes of the Creator in His Majesty while witnessing this orderly universe, which continually changes in systematic, purposive ways and is ceaselessly renewed in a similar orderly manner? Denying the Creator means believing that every existent thing has God-like powers.

For example, an air atom somehow knows how to enter and work upon a flower, a fruit, or a leaf, for it can do so only if it knows the structure and form of all objects it penetrates and affects. Does it have that all-encompassing power and knowledge attributable only to God? Or, a soil atom enables countless different seeds to grow. Either it is acting under Divine command or it has the means and instruments appropriate to all trees and plants. Does each soil atom know each plant's structure and all forms or have the power and artistry to fashion those forms? No. This also is true for all other levels and realms of creation.

There are many clear evidences of God's Unity in all things. To create everything from one thing, and to make everything into one thing, requires a Power available only to the Creator of all. So, pay heed: *There is nothing but glorifies Him with praise* (17:44). If you reject a Single, Peerless God, you must accept as many gods as there are created beings.

SECOND INDICATION: The parable that we mentioned earlier cited a most noble commander. We pointed out that those who see his decorations and medals must know he is the king's favored servant who acts according to the king's commands. This commander is God's Most Noble Messenger.[8] The All-Holy, the Creator of so beautiful a universe, must send a noble Messenger, just as the sun must emit light. The sun cannot exist without emitting light, and Divinity cannot be without revealing itself by sending Prophets.

Could an absolute, perfect beauty not will to present itself through one who would demonstrate and display it? Could that perfectly beautiful artistry not will to make itself known through one who will draw our attention to it? Could the universal dominion of an all-embracing Lordship not will to make known its being One and the Eternally-Besought-of-All to all levels of multiplicity and particularity through a Messenger ennobled by his double authority? His worship's universality makes him the Realm of Multiplicity's envoy to the Divine Court, and his nearness to God and his being entrust-

---

[8] In any publication dealing with Prophet Muhammad, his name or title is followed by "upon him be peace and blessings," to show our respect for him and because it is a religious requirement. For his Companions and other illustrious Muslims: "May God be pleased with him (or her)" is used. However, as this might be distracting to non-Muslim readers, these phrases do not appear in this book, on the understanding that they are assumed and that no disrespect is intended. (Ed.)

ed with His Message make him the Divine Court's envoy to that realm.

Could the One of infinite essential Beauty not will to behold, and have others behold in many mirrors, His Beauty's aspects and His Grace's dimensions? His beloved Messenger holds up a mirror to Him via his worship. The bearer of God's Message, he makes God Almighty beloved by us and shows us His Names' beauty.

Could the Owner of treasuries filled with extraordinary miracles and priceless goods not will to show them to an appreciative humanity via the expert skills of a master jeweler and his descriptive eloquence, thereby revealing His hidden perfections? Could the One Who shows His Names' perfection in a universe so adorned that it resembles a palace decorated with every variety of subtle, miraculous artistry not appoint a teacher and guide so that humanity might understand the wonders of His creation?

Could the Lord Who rules and sustains the universe not resolve, by means of His Messenger, our bewilderment over why there is constant change in the universe, and answer the questions on everyone's mind: What is our origin? Where are we headed? What is our purpose [here]? Could the Majestic Maker, Who makes Himself known to conscious beings through His fair creation and loved through His precious gifts, not send a Messenger to convey to them what His Will demands from them in exchange? Could God create us with a disposition to suffer from multiplicity (this world and its charms) alongside an ability to engage in universal worship, without simultaneously wanting us to turn away from multiplicity and toward Unity by means of a teacher and guide?

Prophethood has many other functions, each of which is a decisive argument that Divinity necessarily implies Messengership. Has there ever been a person more worthy and qualified to fulfil these functions, more fitted to the rank of Messenger, more suited to the task of conveying God's Message, than Prophet Muhammad? No. He is the master of Messengers, the foremost of Prophets, the leader of purified scholars, the nearest to God of those who have drawn near to Him, the most perfect of creatures, and the master of those who guide to righteousness.

Leaving aside the countless indications of his Prophethood seen in his recorded miracles and confirmed by all scholars, the supreme miracle of the Qur'an—an ocean of truth and a miraculous book in 40 different aspects—alone establishes his Prophethood. Since we discussed these aspects elsewhere,[9] we limit our discussion here.

THIRD INDICATION: Is our rank too lowly and our being too trivial for this immense creation to be replaced only so we can be brought to account? No, for our slightness is only apparent. Our comprehensive nature makes us the master of all creatures and endows us with the capacity to herald God's Dominion and offer Him universal worship. Given this, we are the most important being in creation.

If someone asks how such a transient being can deserve eternal punishment, consider that unbelief strives to make creation, which is as invaluable and exalted as a letter written by God, meaningless and pointless. It rejects the manifestations, imprints, and inscriptions of the His Holy Names, which are evident in all that is. It also seeks to deny the infinite proofs showing the truth of God. In short, unbelief insults existence and thus is a crime

---

[9] Particularly in The Twenty-fifth Word.

of infinite proportions deserving infinite punishment.

FOURTH INDICATION: The parable in the Twelve Pictures argued that a king who controlled one realm like a transient hostelry necessarily must have another, an eternal and permanent realm in which the majesty and sublimity of his being king are properly displayed. It is also impossible that the Eternal Creator of this transient world would not create an eternal realm; that the Maker of this beautiful but mutable universe, Himself Everlasting, would not create another permanent and everlasting universe; that the All-Wise, All-Powerful, All-Merciful Creator of a world that is like an arena of trial and exhibition, would not create a Hereafter in which this world's purposes are manifested appropriately. The way into this truth consists of twelve gates that can be unlocked via twelve other truths. We begin with the shortest and simplest one.

FIRST TRUTH: The gate of Lordship and Sovereignty, the manifestation of His Name the All-Sustaining Lord and Master. Would the Glory of God's being the Lord and Divine Sovereign create this temporary universe to display His perfections, with such noble aims and purposes, without also establishing a reward for believers who, by belief and worship, seek to satisfy them? Should He not punish those misguided people who reject His purposes?

SECOND TRUTH: The gate of Munificence and Mercy, the manifestations of His Names the All-Munificent and All-Merciful. Would the Lord of this world, Who demonstrates infinite munificence, mercy, splendor, and glory through His works, recompense according to His Muni-ficence and Mercy and punish according to His Splendor and Glory?

Consider the following: All animate beings are given some form of appropriate sustenance.[10] The weakest and most powerless receive the best sustenance. Such bountiful largesse given with such noble magnanimity betokens a giving hand of Infinite

---

[10] All allowed nourishment is obtained through neediness. The decisive argument for this is how powerless infants enjoy the best livelihood, while strong, wild beasts suffer all kinds of want; how unintelligent fish grow fat, while cunning foxes and monkeys grow thin, in quest of their livelihood. There appears to be an inverse relationship between sustenance received on the one hand, and force and will on the other. The more one relies on force and will, the greater difficulty he or she will have in obtaining sustenance.

Munificence. During spring, all trees are dressed in silk-like finery, covered with blossoms and fruits as if bejeweled, and made to offer many varieties of the choicest fruits on their branches, stretched forward like a servant's arms. We receive sweet and wholesome honey from a stinging honeybee, dress in the finest and softest cloth woven by a handless silkworm, and find a great treasure of Mercy stored for us in tiny seeds. Who but One having the most perfect Munificence, the finest and most subtle Mercy, can do such things?

Except for humanity [and jinn] and certain wild animals, all creatures perform their tasks with complete exactitude, do not overstep their bounds, and are perfectly obedient in an atmosphere of solemn awe. This shows that they function by the command of One having Supreme Majesty and Authority. Similarly, the way all mothers in the vegetable, animal, and human realms support their helpless infants by tenderly and compassionately nurturing their growth with milk shows the all-embracing Mercy.[11]

---

[11] A hungry lion can prefer its offspring to itself and let it eat the meat that normally it would have eaten. A timid rabbit can challenge a lion to protect its young. A fig tree contents itself with mud while feeding its offspring (its fruit) on pure "milk." Thus they obey the One of Infinite Mercy, Munificence,

The Majestic Lord and Ruler of this world has infinite Munificence and Mercy, infinite Splendor and Majesty. His munificence requires infinite giving, His mercy requires favoring worthy of itself, and His majesty and splendor require chastizing those who disrespect them. As only a minute fraction of such attributes are established and manifested in this impermanent world and passing life, there must be a blessed realm that can fulfill these duties. Denying such a realm means denying the Mercy so evident to us, which would be like denying the sun whose existence lightens every day. Death without resurrection would turn compassion into torment, love into the affliction of separation, blessing into a vengeful curse, reason into an instrument of wretchedness, and pleasure into pain. Such events would cause Divine Mercy to vanish.

There also must be a realm of punishment suitable for the Almighty's Majesty and Glory. This world's oppressors die with their oppressive pow-

---

and Solicitousness. Likewise, the fact that unconscious plants and beasts act in the most purposive and conscious manner shows irrefutably that One All-Knowing and All-Wise has set them to their tasks, and that they act in His Name.

er intact, while the oppressed die still subjected to humiliation. Such wrongs necessarily are deferred to a supreme tribunal; they are never ignored. Indeed, punishment is sometimes enacted even in this world. The torments endured by earlier disobedient and rebellious peoples show that we cannot escape whatever correction God Almighty's Splendor and Majesty chooses to apply.

Why should humanity refuse to recognize Him and respond to Him in belief, for we have the highest duty in creation and so are blessed with the most important capacities. In addition, our Lord and Sustainer reveals Himself through His orderly works. Why should humanity not respond to Him by making ourselves beloved of God through worship, for He makes Himself loved by us for the numerous, adorned gifts of His Mercy. Why should humanity not respond to Him with reverent thanks and praise, for He shows His Love and Mercy to us through the gifts of His Grace.

Does it make sense that we should remain unrecompensed and unanswerable, that the Majestic One of Splendor and Glory should not prepare a realm of requital for us? Does it make sense that the All-Merciful and Compassionate One would not prepare a realm of permanent reward and bliss for believers who respond to His making Himself known by recognizing Him in belief, to His making Himself beloved by loving Him in worship, and to His Mercy by offering reverent thanks and praise?

THIRD TRUTH: The gate of Wisdom and Justice, the manifestations of His Names the All-Wise and All-Just.[12] Would the Majestic Being, Who manifests the sovereignty of His being Lord in the universe's order, purposiveness, justice, and balance, not show His favor to believers who seek the protection of His being their Lord and Sovereign, who

---

[12] In this and other arguments, such interrogative words and phrases as *could, would, is it conceivable,* and *does it make sense* are reiterated to point to a very significant truth: Misguidance and a lack of belief often arise from the habit of imagining things to be impossible or beyond sense and then denying them. In our discussion of the Resurrection, we argued emphatically that the real impossibility, absurdity, and irrationality come along the path of unbelief and misguidance, whereas real possibility, facility, and rationality are characteristics of the broad highway of belief (Islam). In sum, materialist and naturalist philosophers veer into unbelief by regarding possibilities as impossible, whereas The Tenth Word, by using such words as mentioned above, points to where the impossibility really is.

believe in His Wisdom and Justice, and act in conformity with them through worship? Would He not chastise those who, denying His Wisdom and Justice, rebel against Him? Since only a minute amount of His Wisdom and Justice with respect to humanity is established in this transient world, they must be deferred. Most of the misguided die unpunished, and most of the guided die unrewarded. Such affairs certainly are deferred to a supreme tribunal, an ultimate contentment.

The One Who administers this world does so in accordance with an infinite wisdom. We can see this in how all things are used and benefit others. Have you not seen how many wise purposes are served by each human limb, bone, and vein, as well as by every brain cell and every cell atom in your body? Indeed, the purposes are as numerous as a tree's fruits. This confirms that all is arranged in accordance with infinite wisdom. A further proof is the absolute orderliness in which everything is fashioned.

The miniaturization of the whole, exact program of a flower's growth in a tiny seed, as well as the Pen of Destiny's making a large tree's seed the index of its life-history and all its parts, show that an absolute wisdom moves that Pen. The perfection of subtle artistry in all things proves an infinitely Wise Artist's impress. Including an index of all beings within a small human body, as well as the keys to Mercy's treasuries and mirrors to reflect all Divine Names, further shows the Wisdom within that infinitely subtle artistry. Could this Wisdom, which so permeates the workings of Lordship, not want to favor those who eternally seek refuge in that Lordship's protection and who offer obedience in belief?

Do you need convincing that everything is done with justice and balance? The fact that all things are given being and form, and then placed according to a precise equilibrium and measure, is enough proof for you. The fact that everything receives whatever it needs in the most fitting form, according to its nature, is a sign left by a hand of infinite justice. Every petition and plea voiced in the tongue of disposition, of natural need or necessity, also demonstrates infinite justice and wisdom.

Is it conceivable that the justice and wisdom hastening to provide for creation's smallest member would not provide the greatest need (immortality) of its most important member (humanity)?

Is it conceivable that it would fail to respond to our greatest plea and cry for help, or that it would not preserve the dignity of God's being Lord by rewarding His servants? We cannot experience the true essence of justice in this transient world, for our lives are too short. Thus the affair is deferred to a supreme tribunal.

The true essence of justice requires that we be rewarded and punished not according to our apparent insignificance, but according to the greatness of our wrong and our nature, and the importance of our function. Since this transient world cannot manifest such an amount of wisdom and justice, as humanity is created for eternity, there must be an eternal Hell and an everlasting Paradise created by the All-Just and All-Wise to befit His Grace and Awe.

FOURTH TRUTH: The gate of Generosity and Beauty, the manifestation of the Names the Generous and the Beautiful. Would unlimited generosity and liberality, inexhaustible riches and treasures, unequalled eternal beauty and grace, as well as everlasting perfection, not demand the existence of grateful supplicants, along with amazed and yearning onlookers, destined to dwell permanently in an abode of blissful repose? The world is adorned with so many beautiful objects, the sun and moon serve as its lamps, the planet's surface teems with the finest varieties of sustenance—an overflowing feast of plenty, trees bearing fruit like so many dishes and renewed several times each season. All of this shows the existence of unlimited generosity and liberality.

Such inexhaustible treasures of Mercy require an everlasting abode of blissful repose that contains all desirable objects. They also require that those who enjoy it should dwell there eternally, without suffering the pain of cessation and separation. The end of pain is a sort of pleasure, and the end of pleasure is a sort of pain. As unlimited generosity cannot allow such a thing, Paradise must be eternal and its inhabitants must live therein eternally. Unlimited generosity and liberality desire to bestow infinite bounty and kindness, which require infinite gratitude. Thus, those who are to receive and give continual thanks for this ongoing bestowal of bounty must live forever. A slight contentment, spoiled by its brevity or cessation, is incompatible with unlimited generosity and liberality.

Reflect upon the world's different regions, how each exhibits God's handiwork and proclaims His being Lord in the diversity of all plants and animals.[13] Listen to the Prophets and saints who proclaim His Lordship's beauties. They point to the Majestic Maker's flawless perfections and demonstrate His miraculous arts, thereby inviting our admiration.

The Maker of this world wishes to make His most important, amazing, and hidden perfections known via His miraculous arts. Hidden perfection longs to be known by those who will gaze upon it with admiration and appreciation. Eternal perfection requires eternal manifestation, which in turn requires the eternal existence of those who will appreciate and admire it. The value of perfection diminishes in the view of its admirer if the latter is not eternal.[14]

---

[13] A brilliantly shaped, a dazzlingly domed flower, a most artfully wrought jewel-like fruit on a twig as fine as wire and attached to a tree's rigid bough—such things proclaim the fine artistry of a most skilled, wise, and miraculous fashioner to all animate beings. The same is true of the animal and plant kingdoms.

[14] A celebrated beauty once rejected a common man who had become infatuated with her. To console himself, the man said:

The brilliant adornment and beautiful handiwork of all Earth's creatures testify to the dimensions of an unequaled transcendent Grace and point to the subtle aspects of a hidden Beauty, just as sunlight testifies to the sun's existence.[15] Every manifestation of that transcendent Beauty, that holy Grace, points to the existence of innumerable unseen treasures in each of God's Names. So exalted, peerless, and hidden a beauty wills to behold itself in a mirror, to see its degrees and measures reflected in animate beings, and to become manifest so that it may look upon itself through the eyes of others.

In short, beauty and grace will to see and be seen and thus require the existence of yearning witnesses and dazzled admirers. Since Divine Beauty is

---

"How ugly she is!" and so denied her beauty. A bear once stood beneath a vine trellis and longed to eat the grapes upon it. Unable to reach the grapes or to climb the trellis, he said to himself, by way of consolation: "The grapes must be sour," and went on his way growling.

[15] While all beings that act as mirrors for Divine Beauty continually depart and disappear, others succeed them, manifesting in their forms and features the same Beauty. This shows that such Beauty does not belong to them; rather, the visible instances of beauty are the signs and indications of a transcendent, holy Beauty.

eternal and everlasting, its witnesses and admirers also must be eternal, for Eternal Beauty can never be content with transient admirers. The love of an admirer condemned to permanent separation will turn to hatred once the thought of separation takes hold. Admiration yields to an ill opinion, and respect yields to contempt. Just as obstinate people may be enemies of what they do not know, they are opposed to what lies beyond their reach. A finite love responds to a beauty that deserves infinite admiration with tacit hostility, hatred, and rejection. This is a profound reason for why unbelievers hate God.

Such unlimited generosity and liberality, unequalled beauty and absolute perfection require the existence of suppliants and admirers with eternal longing and gratitude. But this temporary world's inhabitants depart having tasted that generosity only long enough to whet their appetites. Seeing only a dim shadow of perfection's light, they are not fully content. Thus we can be sure that we are traveling to a place of eternal joy where we will receive what we are due in full measure. In short, just as this world and its creatures prove the Majestic

Creator's existence, His holy Attributes and Names point to and necessitate the Hereafter's existence.

FIFTH TRUTH: The gate of Compassion and the Prophet's sincere acts of worship, the manifestation of the Names the Answerer of Prayer and the Compassionate. Is it conceivable that a Lord of infinite compassion and mercy, Who most compassionately fulfills the least need of His lowliest creatures in the most unexpected fashion, Who answers the faintest cry of help of His most obscure creature, and Who responds to all petitions would ignore the greatest petition of His foremost servant, his most beloved creature, by not granting his most exalted prayer?

The tender solicitude manifested in nurturing weak, young animals show that the Sovereign Lord of the universe exercises His being Lord with infinite mercy. Is it conceivable that such compassion and mercy in the exercise of Lordship would refuse the prayer of the most virtuous and beautiful of all creation?[16] This great truth is explained in The

---

[16] Namely, the Prophet, who has ruled for 14 centuries over billions of subjects who daily renew their allegiance to him, continually bear witness to his perfections, and fully obey his commands. His spiritual temperament has shaped one-half

Nineteenth Word, but we reiterate the argument here.

We mentioned in the parable a meeting held in a certain land, at which a most noble commander spoke. To discover this parable's truth, imagine that we can return to the Arabian peninsula during the blessed age of the Prophet, and visit and watch him perform his duties and worship. He is the means to attaining eternal happiness, since he is the Messenger and the one with guidance, as well as the reason for that happiness' creation—the creation of Paradise—through his worship and prayer.

See how he is praying for eternal happiness with such perfect supplication and sublime worship. It is as if the peninsula, indeed the whole world, were praying and supplicating with him, for his

of the globe and one-fourth of humanity. He is the beloved of humanity's hearts, the guide of their souls, and the greatest servant of the Lord of the worlds. Since most of the realms of created beings applaud the duty and role entrusted to him through each bearing the fruit of his miracles, he is the most beloved creature of the Creator of all. Further, the desire for permanence and continuance implanted in our nature, which lifts us from the lowest to the highest rank, is the greatest desire and petition, and can be presented to the Provider of all needs only by His greatest servant.

worship contains his community's worship, as well as the essentials of all other Prophets' worship, for they all obeyed the same One Lord.

He offers his supreme prayer and supplications amid so many beings that it is as if all illustrious and perfect people, from the time of Adam to the present, were following him in prayer and saying "Amen" to his petition.[17] He is petitioning for so universal a need—immortality—that all inhabitants of creation share in it and silently affirm: "Accept his prayer, O Lord, because we also desire it." He pleads for everlasting happiness so plaintively, with such yearning and longing, that creation is moved to tears and shares in his plea.

See how he desires and prays for happiness. Such a purpose and goal raises all creatures from

---

[17] From the Prophet's first petition until now, all invocations upon him of peace and blessings resemble a continual "Amen" after his prayer, a universal participation. Al-Shafi'i writes that each such invocation during one's prayers, and the prayer for him after the second call to worship during the prescribed prayers, is a powerful and universal "Amen" to his plea for eternal happiness. The eternity and everlasting happiness so strongly desired by humanity, in accord with its primordial nature, is desired for them by the Prophet, and the illustrious segment of humanity says after him: "Amen!" Could such a universal petition not be granted?

the abyss of annihilation, worthless and aimless futility, to the summit of worth, exalted purpose, and eternal life. It makes everything reach the station of being a script written by God, the Eternally-Besought-of-All. His petition is so noble, an asking for mercy so sweet, that it is as if he inspired all beings, the heavens, and the Divine Throne to hear and echo his words with ecstatic cries of "Amen, O Lord, Amen!"[18]

---

[18] Could the Master of this world, all of Whose acts are self-evidently based on His absolute Awareness, Knowledge, and Wisdom, be unaware and uninformed of his foremost creature's deeds and prayers, remain indifferent to them, or consider them unimportant? Being aware and not indifferent, could the All-Powerful and All-Merciful Sovereign of the world not accept his prayers? The light of Muhammad has changed the world's form. The true essence of humanity and of all beings in the universe became apparent through that light; namely, that each is a missive of the Eternally Besought One proclaiming the Divine Names; a valued, meaningful being with God-given functions and destined for eternity. Were it not for that light, beings would be condemned to annihilation; without worth, meaning, or use; bewildered effects of blind chance and lost in the blackness of illusion. That is why just as humanity says "Amen" to the Prophet's prayer, all other beings from Earth's surface to the Divine Throne, from underground to above the stars, take pride in his light and proclaim their connection with him. The very spirit of the Prophet's

He asks for eternal happiness from One, the All-Generous and All-Powerful, the All-Seeing, Merciful and All-Knowing, Who visibly sees, hears, accepts, and pities the most hidden wish and least desire of His most obscure creature. He answers all pleas and bestows His favors with a Mercy so wise and apt that no one can doubt that the one who does these is the One All-Hearing and All-Seeing, Generous and Merciful.

For what is the pride of all being petitioning? He is humanity's fountain of honor, the unique individual who stands on this Earth with all humanity behind him and with his hands opened toward God's Throne and prays. In reality, his worship and servanthood to God includes our worship and is the essence of it. He asks for eternal happiness for himself and all believers, for eternity and Paradise. He petitions through and with all sacred Divine Names, Whose beauty is reflected in all created beings. Surely you see that he is seeking intercession from those Names. Even if there were not

_____

petition is this prayer for everlasting happiness. All of the universe's motions and workings are in essence prayer, just as, for example, a seed's growth until it becomes a tree is a form of prayer to the All-Sustaining Creator.

innumerable other reasons and causes for it, a single prayer of his would suffice for creating Paradise, a task as easy for the All-Merciful's power as creating spring.

How could creating Paradise be difficult for One All-Powerful, Who each spring makes Earth's surface a vast field of renewal and brings forth countless resurrections? Just as the Prophet's being the Messenger was the reason for establishing this realm of trial as mentioned in a hadith qudsi—*But for you, I would not have created the worlds* is an indication of this—his worship was the cause for establishing the abode of happiness.

Would the perfect artistry and unequalled beauty of God's being Lord, seen in creation's amazing orderliness and comprehensive mercy, refuse the Prophet's prayer and thereby allow extreme ugliness, pitilessness, and discord? Would the All-Sustaining Lord hear and grant the most insignificant desire but refuse the greatest and most important desire as worthless? No, He would not! Such Beauty could never countenance such ugliness and thereby make itself ugly. Just as the Prophet opened this world's gates by being God's Messenger, he opens the Hereafter's gates by worshipping Him.

Upon him be the blessings of the All-Merciful One, to the extent of that which fills this world and the abode of gardens—Paradise. O God, bestow blessings and peace on Your servant and Messenger, that beloved one who is the master of both realms, the pride of all worlds, the source of life in both worlds, the means for attaining happiness here and in the Hereafter, one who combines Prophethood and Messengership in himself, who preached the principles of a happy life in this world and the next, who is the Messenger of humanity and jinn—on him, his Family, all his Companions, as well as his fellow Prophets and Messengers. Amen.

SIXTH TRUTH: The gate of Majesty and Eternity, the manifestation of the Names the All-Majestic and the All-Permanent. Is it conceivable that the majesty in His being the Lord, to Whose command all beings are subdued like obedient soldiers, should focus entirely upon the transient beings in this temporary world, and not create a permanent sphere for itself to eternally manifest His being Lord? The Divine majesty seen in seasonal changes, the planets' sublime circling as if they were aircraft, everything's orderliness, Earth's creation as our cradle and the sun as our lamp, and such vast transformations as reviving and adorning a dry, dead Earth—

all of these show that a sublime Lordship, a majestic Sovereignty, rules behind the veil of what is seen.

That infinite, glorious Sovereignty requires subjects worthy of itself, as well as a fitting vehicle for its manifestation. But humanity, the world's most important inhabitant and blessed with the most comprehensive functions, is gathered to stay here only for a limited while and is in a pitiable state. The world is filled and emptied daily, as well as transformed hourly, and we stay only temporarily to be tested in service. All of the Sovereign's subjects are like would-be buyers who come for a while to view samples of the precious gifts bestowed by the Majestic Maker, His miraculous works of art in the showcase of this world. They soon leave, while the spectacle changes every minute. Whoever departs never returns, and whoever comes eventually departs.

Such a reality argues that behind and beyond this world and its activities is a permanent, eternal abode that fully manifests God's everlasting Sovereignty—palaces, gardens, treasure houses stocked with the pure and perfect originals of the forms and copies we see here. We strive here for what awaits us there. We labor here and are rewarded there. Bliss awaits all, provided that they are not among the losers, and is enjoyed according to each person's capacity. In short, an Eternal Sovereignty cannot focus exclusively upon a realm whose transience makes it wretched.

Consider this analogy: While travelling, you see a caravanserai built by a great person for those coming to visit him. Decorated at the greatest expense, it delights and instructs the guests during their night's stay. They see only a little of those decorations, and only for a very short time. Having briefly tasted the joys of what is offered, they continue on their journey unsatisfied. How-ever, each guest photographs the objects in the caravanserai, while the great person's servants record every guest's conduct and preserve the record. The guests notice that most of the wonderful decorations are replaced daily with fresh ones for newly arriving guests.

Having seen all this, the only reasonable conclusion is that the caravanserai's owner must have permanent exalted dwellings, inexhaustible and precious treasures, and an uninterrupted flow of unlimited generosity. He shows his generosity in the caravanserai to arouse his guests' appetite for what he keeps in his immediate presence, and to awaken their desire for the gifts prepared for them.

If you reflect upon this world with an unclouded concentration, you will understand the Nine Principles explained below:

- **First principle:** This world (the caravanserai) neither exists or assumed this shape by itself. Rather, it is a well-constructed hostelry, wisely designed to receive the caravan of beings that constantly arrive, stay for awhile, and then leave.

- **Second principle:** We are guests here, invited to the Abode of Peace by our Generous Sustainer.

- **Third principle:** This world's adornments are meant to rouse our appetite. As they are temporary and give pain upon separation, they are here only to instruct in wisdom, arouse gratitude, and encourage us to seek the permanent originals of which they are copies.[19] In short, they are exalted goals far beyond themselves.

---

[19] The lifespan of all worldly things is short, whereas their worth and the subtleties in their fashioning are most exalted and beautiful. This implies that everything is only a sample to draw the viewer's gaze to its authentic original. Given this, we may say that this world's diverse adornments are

- **Fourth principle:** The world's adornments are like samples and forms of the blessings stored in Paradise by the All-Merciful's Mercy for people of belief.[20]

samples of Paradise's bounties, made ready by the Compassionate and Merciful One for His beloved servants.

[20] Everything exists for many purposes, and numerous effects result from it. These purposes and effects are not, as the misguided suppose, related only to this world and to humanity; rather, they relate to these three categories:

The first and the most exalted pertains to the Creator: to present to His gaze the splendidly adorned wonders He has attached to each thing, as if for a military parade to which He is the Pre-Eternal Witness. The most fleeting existence suffices to attain His glance. Indeed, the mere potentiality for existence suffices. This purpose is fully realized, for example, by fragile creatures that swiftly perish, and by seeds and kernels, each a masterpiece, that never flower or bear fruit. Such creatures remain untouched by vanity and futility. The primary purpose of all things is to proclaim, by their very being, the miracles of their Maker's Power and signs of His handiwork, and to show them to His gaze.

The second category pertains to conscious beings. Every thing is like a truth-bearing missive, or artistic poem, or a wise word of the Majestic Maker offered to angels and jinn, humanity and animals, and desiring to be "read" by them. Every thing is an object for the contemplation and instruction of every conscious being that looks upon it.

The third category relates to the things' selves, and consists of such minor effects as the experience of pleasure and joy,

- **Fifth principle:** All transient things were created to be assembled briefly in existence and

---

of abiding with some degree of permanence and comfort. If
we consider the functions of a steersman employed on a
royal yacht, we see that only 1% of those functions actually relate to the steersman (e.g., his wages); the other 99%
relate to the king who owns the yacht. A similar proportion
obtains between the things' purposes related to its self and
worldly existence and those related to its Maker.

Given this multiplicity of purposes, we can explain the
ultimate correlation between Divine Wisdom and economy,
as well as Divine Liberality and Generosity (which are in reality unlimited), even though they seem to contradict each other. In the individual purposes of things, liberality and generosity predominate and the Name the Most Generous is manifested. For example, fruits and grains are beyond reckon-
ing and manifest the Name the Most Generous. But in the
universal purposes things are made to serve, the Name the All-
Wise is manifested. It may be said that a fruit of a tree has
as many purposes as the number of its fruits. These purposes can be divided into the three categories just mentioned.

The universal purposes demonstrate an infinite wisdom
and economy. Infinite wisdom and infinite generosity are thus
correlated, despite their apparent opposition. For example,
one purpose for raising an army is to maintain order. The troops
already available may be enough to achieve this. However,
the whole army may be barely enough for such other purposes as protecting national frontiers and repelling enemies.
Wisdom and multiplicity are thus correlated, just as the purpose
of a government's existence never contradicts its splendor.

to acquire their requisite forms so that they can be registered, their images preserved, their meanings understood, and their consequences recorded. This is so that, among other purposes in the Realm of Permanence, everlasting spectacles might be wrought from them for the people of eternity. Everything has been created for eternity, not for annihilation.

Apparent annihilation marks a completion of duty and a release from service, for while every transient thing progresses to annihilation in one aspect, it remains eternally in many other aspects. Consider a flower, a word of God's Power. It smiles upon us for a while and then hides behind the veil of annihilation. It disappears just as a spoken word does: it is gone, but its meaning remains in the minds of those who heard it. The flower is gone, but it leaves its visible form in the memory of those who saw it and its inner essence in its sees. It is as if each memory and seed were a device to record the flower's adornment or a means for its perpetuation.

As this is true for such a simple entity, we can see how much closer we are attached to eternity, given that we are life's highest form and have an imperishable soul. Again, from the fact that the laws according to which flowering and fruit-bearing plants are formed, and that representations of their forms are preserved and perpetuated in the most orderly manner in tiny seeds through all tempestuous changes [of weather, seasons, and the like], we can understand easily how closely each person's spirit is attached and related to eternity.[21] This spirit, which gives each person a most exalted and comprehensive nature, is like a conscious and luminous law issuing from the Divine Command despite its being housed in a body.

- **Sixth principle:** We have not been left to wander at will, like a loosely tethered animal pasturing where it pleases. Our deeds' forms and consequences are recorded, registered, and preserved for the Day when we will have to account for them.

- **Seventh principle:** The wholesale death of spring and summer creatures during autumn is not an annihilation, but a dismissal after the duty's completion, an emptying that makes way

---

[21] These laws have the same meaning for the life and existence of plants as a spirit has for the individual human being.

for new creatures to come next spring and assume their functions.[22] It is a Divine warning to rouse conscious beings from their forgetfulness, to shake them out of the torpor that causes them to neglect their duty to give thanks.

- **Eighth principle:** This transient world's Eternal Maker has an eternal world toward which He urges and impels His servants.

- **Ninth principle:** In that world, One so Compassionate will give the best of His servants gifts that are so far beyond our knowledge that we cannot imagine them. In this we believe.

SEVENTH TRUTH: The gate of Protection and Preservation, the display of the Names the All-

---

[22] It is fitting that a tree's leaves, flowers, and fruits, which are sustained by Divine Mercy, depart when their time is over and their duties ended. Otherwise the gate open to those following them would block the expansion of God's Mercy and the services to be performed by the species' other members. Also, they become wretched and distressed when they pass their prime. Spring is like a fruit-bearing tree indicating the vast Plain of Resurrection. Similarly, in every age this world is like a tree inviting contemplation; the world as a whole is like a wonderful tree whose fruits are sent ahead to the market of the Hereafter.

Preserver and the Guardian. Is it conceivable that God's attribute of Preserver, protecting within absolute orderliness and equilibrium all that exists, and sifting and accounting their consequences, would allow the acts of His noble vicegerent, who bears the Supreme Trust, to go unrecorded, unsifted and unaccounted, unweighed in the balance of justice, unpunished or unrewarded fittingly, even though his acts relate so closely to God's universal Lordship?[23] It is not.

The Being Who administers this cosmos preserves all things in an order and balance that manifest His Knowledge and Wisdom, Will and Power. We see that the substance of every created thing, and all its subsequent individual forms and in their totality, are fashioned in perfect (and pleasing, symmetrical) orderliness. Moreover, the Majestic Preserver preserves many forms of things that perish after finishing their duties and departing, in people's memories, which are like a Supreme Preserved Tablet

---

[23] God's vicegerency means that humanity is the "means" God "uses" to execute His commands on Earth and that we rule it according to His laws. The Supreme Trust is our ego, which has been equipped, relatively, with all manifestations of Divine Names and Attributes. Also, see The Thirtieth Word. (Tr.)

or archetypal mirror. He inscribes a compact life-history in a seed (that life's issue and outcome). Thus He causes all things to be preserved in mirrors corresponding to outer and inner worlds. Human memories, a tree's fruit, a fruit's kernel, a flower's seed—all manifest the law of preservation's universality and inclusiveness.

Have you not seen how the records of the deeds of all spring flowers and fruits, laws of their formation, and images of their forms are all inscribed within a minute seed and there preserved? The following spring, those records are opened—a bringing to account appropriate to them—and another vast world of spring emerges with absolute orderliness and wisdom. This shows the powerful and comprehensive exercise of the Divine Attribute of Preserver. Considering that the issue of such transient, commonplace, and insignificant things is preserved, how could our deeds, which (from the viewpoint of universal Lordship) yield important fruit in the Unseen world, the Hereafter, and the World of Spirits, not be preserved and recorded as a matter of high significance?

This comprehensive preserving shows us what great care the Master of creation devotes to the orderliness of everything that occurs under His Rule. He is absolutely attentive to the function of being Sovereign and Sustainer and Lord. Therefore He records, or causes to be recorded, the least event and smallest service and preserves everything's form in numerous records. This attribute of Preserver indicates that the records of our deeds will be laid open and closely scrutinized and weighed.

Ennobled with God's vicegerency and Trust, we are witnesses to the universality of His being Lord and proclaim His Unity in this Realm of Multiplicity. Thus we act as controls and witnesses who enjoy a share in His glorification and the worship of most beings. How can we do all of this and then be consigned to an endless sleep in the grave, never to be roused and questioned about what we did? Without a doubt, we will travel to the Plain of Resurrection and be tried at the Supreme Tribunal.

We cannot flee or hide in nothingness or enter the ground, just as we cannot conceal ourselves from the All-Powerful and Majestic One to Whose Power all future contingencies and all past events bear witness, and Who creates winter and spring which, taken together, resemble the Resurrection.[24] Since we are not properly called to account and judged while in this world, we must proceed to a Supreme Tribunal and lasting happiness in another.

---

[24] The past consists of events. Every day, year, and century that came into being is like a line, a page, and a book inscribed by the Pen of Destiny. Divine Power inscribes Its miraculous works in it in perfect wisdom and orderliness. Similarly, the future, from now until the Resurrection, Paradise, and eternity, consists entirely of contingencies. Comparing these two, we understand with certainty that the Being Who created yesterday and its creatures can create tomorrow and its creatures. As past wonders are the miraculous works of a Powerful and Majestic One, they affirm that He can create the future and its contingencies and show its wonders.

The One Who creates an apple certainly can create all apples and bring spring into being. Equally, one who cannot create spring cannot create a single apple, for they are made at the same workbench. Each apple is a miniature example of a tree, a garden, or a cosmos. Its seed carries within itself the tree's life-history, and displays such perfect artistry that it is a miracle created by the One Who can do anything. Likewise, the One Who creates today can create the Day of Resurrection, and only He Who can create spring can create the Resurrection. The One Who threads all past events on the ribbon of time and displays them there in perfect wisdom and order can attach other beings to the ribbon of the future and display them there. In several treatises of *The Words*, we proved that the One Who can create one thing can

EIGHTH TRUTH: The gate of Promise and Threat, the display of the Names the Beautiful and the Majestic. Would the Maker of this world, Who has Absolute Knowledge and Absolute Power, not fulfill the oft-repeated promise and threat affirmed by all Prophets, truth seekers, and saints? Not doing so would show impotence or ignorance. His Power can realize His promise and threat as easily as He brings back in spring the innumerable beings of the spring before, some identical (the roots of trees and grass) and some similar (leaves and fruits). Our need for everything, and the requirement of His being Sovereign and Lord, means He will fulfill His promise. Not doing so would contradict His Power's dignity and authority and His Knowledge's comprehensiveness.

If you deny such facts, in reality you are following your own lying fancy, capricious intellect, and deceiving soul. You call Him a liar, though He never breaks His promise, for His Glory and Dignity

---

create everything. Also, if everything's creation is attributed to a Single Being, their creation becomes as easy as creating one thing. But if creation is attributed to multiple agents or causes, the creation of one thing is as hard as creating everything. As a result, it borders on the impossible.

make this impossible for Him. Moreover, His truthfulness is attested to by everything you see. Despite your insignificance, your error is infinite and thus deserving of a great and eternal punishment.[25] Those who deny resemble travelers who close their eyes to sunlight and turn to the light of their own fantasies, although it is no stronger than a glowworm's, to light the awful road ahead. The Almighty does what He promises. His truthful words are these beings we see, and His truthful, eloquent signs are the processes of nature. And so He will establish a Supreme Tribunal and bestow everlasting happiness.

NINTH TRUTH: The gate of God's revival and causing death, the manifestation of the Names the Ever-Living and the Self-Subsistent, the One Who Revives and the One Who Causes To Die. God revives this vast Earth when it is dead and dry, thereby displaying His Power via quickening countless species of creation, each as extraordinary as humanity. He shows His all-embracing Knowledge in these creatures' infinite variations within the com-

---

[25] According to certain Traditions, the teeth of some of people in Hell will be as large as mountains, an indication of the size of their error.

plex intermingling of all their distinct forms. God turns His servants' attention toward everlasting contentment, assuring them of resurrection in His heavenly decrees, and makes visible the splendor of His being their Lord and Nurturer. He causes all His creatures to collaborate with each other, turning within the orbit of His Command and Will, and to help each other in submission to Him.

He shows our value by creating us as the Tree of Creation's most comprehensive, subtle, worthiest, and valued, fruit; by addressing us directly and subjugating all things to us. Could One so Compassionate and Powerful, Wise and All-Knowing, not (or be unable to) bring about the resurrection, assemble His creatures, and restore us to life? Could He could not institute His Supreme Court or create Heaven and Hell? Such ideas are inconceivable.

Indeed, the Almighty Disposer of this world's affairs continually creates on its finite, transient surface numerous signs, examples, and indications of the Supreme Gathering and the Plain of Resurrection. Each spring we see countless animal and plant species assembled in a few days and then scattered. All tree and plant roots, as well as certain animals, are revived and restored exactly as they were.

Other animals are re-created in nearly identical forms. Seeds that appear so alike quickly grow into distinct and differentiated entities, after being brought to full vigor with extraordinary rapidity and ease, in absolute orderliness and harmony. How could anything be difficult for the One Who does this? How could He create the heavens and Earth in 6 days and yet be unable to resurrect humanity with a single blast?

Suppose a gifted writer could copy out in an hour the confused, half-effaced letters of countless books on a sheet of paper without error or omission, fully and in the best style. If someone then told you that he could rewrite his own book from memory, even though it had fallen into water and become effaced, how could you say that he could not do so? Or think of a king who, to show his power or warn, removes mountains with a command, turns his kingdom about, and transforms the sea into dry land. Then imagine that a great boulder blocks the path of guests travelling to his reception. If someone says that the king will remove the boulder with a command, would you say that he could not do so?

Or imagine someone assembles a great army, and you are told that he will recall it to parade in battalions by a trumpet blast after dismissing them to rest? If the battalions formed in disciplined rows, would you respond with disbelief? If you did, your error would be enormous.

Now, see how the Eternal Designer closes winter's white page and opens spring's and summer's green pages before our eyes. With the Pen of Power and Destiny, He inscribes infinite species, none of which encroach upon another, on Earth's surface in a most beautiful style. Each has a unique form and shape and is without confusion. The writing also has no error. Is it reasonable to ask the All-Wise and All-Preserving, Who compacts a great tree's being into a dot-sized seed, how He will remove the boulder from the path of travelers coming to meet Him in the Hereafter?

Is it reasonable to ask the All-Glorious, Who inscribes fresh recruits from non-being into His battalions with *Be! and it is,* and with absolute orderliness arranges the ranks of all living things, down to their bodily atoms, and so creates highly disciplined armies—even to ask how He can make bodies submit to His discipline like obedient soldiers, how He can assemble their mutually related fundamental atoms and their members composed thereof?

Can you not see the numerous designs made by God as signs, similitudes, and analogies of resurrection? He has placed them in every era, the alternation of day and night, even in the coming and going of clouds. If you imagine yourself 1,000 years in the past and then compare past and future, you will see as many similitudes and analogies of resurrection as there are centuries and days past. If, after this, you still consider corporeal resurrection improbable and unacceptable to reason, there is something seriously wrong with your powers of reasoning.

Concerning this truth, the Supreme Decree says:

> Look upon the signs and imprints of God's Mercy, how He revives Earth after its death. He it is Who will revive the dead [in the same way]. He is powerful over all things. (30:50)

Nothing makes the Resurrection impossible, and much necessitates it. The glorious and eternal

Lordship, the all-mighty and all-embracing Sovereignty, of the One Who gives life and death to this wide and wonderful Earth as if it were a single organism; Who has made it as a pleasing cradle and handsome craft for humanity and animals; Who has made the sun a lamp that gives it both its light and heat; Who has made the planets transports for His angels—such a One's Lordship and Sovereignty cannot be confined to a mutable, transitory, unstable, slight, and imperfect world.

Thus there is another realm, one worthy of Him, immutable, permanent, stable, great, and perfect. He causes us to work for this realm and summons us to it. Those who have penetrated from outward appearances to truth, who have been ennobled by proximity to the Divine Presence, all spiritual "poles" endowed with light-filled hearts, and those with enlightened minds, testify that He will transfer us to that other kingdom, that He has prepared a reward and a requital for us there, and that He gives us His firm promises and stern warnings thereof.

Breaking a promise is base humiliation and irreconcilable with His Sanctity's glory. Failure to carry out a threat can arise only from forgiveness or impotence. And, unbelief cannot be forgiven.[26] The All-Powerful is exempt from and far above all impotence. All who bring us their testimony agree on this fundamental. In numbers, they have the authority of unanimity; in quality, the authority of learned consensus. In rank, each is a guiding light of humanity, the cherished one of a people and the object of their veneration. In importance, each is a subject expert and authority.

In any art or science, two experts are preferred to thousands of nonexperts, and two positive affirmers are preferred to thousands of negators in a report's transmission. For example, the testimony of two competent men that they have sighted the

---

[26] Unbelief denounces creation, alleging it to be without worth or meaning. It insults creation by denying the manifestation of the Divine Names in the mirrors of created beings. It disrespects the Divine Names, rejects the witness borne to the Unity of God by all beings, and denies creation by so corrupting our potentialities that we cannot reform and become unreceptive to good. Unbelief is also an act of absolute injustice, a transgression against creation and the rights of God's Names. The defense of those rights, and an unbeliever's irredeemable state, require that unbelief be unpardonable. The words *to associate partners with God is truly a great transgression* (31:13) express this necessity.

crescent moon marking the beginning of Ramadan nullifies the negation of thousands of deniers.

This world contains no truer report, firmer claim, or more evident truth than this. It is a field, and the Resurrection—destroying the world and building the Hereafter—is a threshing-floor, a harvesting-ground for grain that will be stored in Paradise or Hell.

TENTH TRUTH: The gate of Wisdom, Grace, Mercy, and Justice, the manifestation of the Names the All-Wise, Munificent, Just, and Merciful. The Majestic Owner of all existence displays such manifest wisdom, pervasive grace, overwhelming justice, and comprehensive mercy in this impermanent world, transitory testing ground, and unstable display hall of Earth.

Is it conceivable that among His realms, in the worlds of existence's outer and inner dimensions, that there would be no permanent abodes with immortal inhabitants residing in everlasting stations? Is it conceivable that even if they did not exist, that all the truths of wisdom, grace, mercy, and justice that we witness should decline into nothingness?

Would the All-Wise choose us to receive His direct and universal address; make us a comprehensive mirror to Himself; let us taste, measure, and get to know the contents of His treasuries of Mercy; make Himself known to us with all His Names; love us and make Himself beloved by us—and then not send us to an eternal realm, an abode of permanent bliss, and make us happy therein? Would He would lay on every being, even a seed, a burden as heavy as a tree, charge it with duties as numerous as flowers, and appoint to it beneficial consequences as numerous as fruits, while assigning to them purposes that are relevant only here?

Why would He restrict His purpose to this worldly life, something less valuable than a grain of a mustard seed? Would it not be more reasonable for Him to make beings in this world as seeds for the immaterial world of meanings and essences, where the true meanings of everything here will be manifested, and as a tillage for the Hereafter, where they will yield their true and worthy produce? Would He really allow such significant alterations (as we witness) to be purposeless, void, and futile? Why would He not turn their faces toward the Immaterial World of Meanings and Essences (where true meanings lie) and the Hereafter, so that they might reveal their true purposes and fitting results there?

If He were to cause things to contradict their own nature, how could He allow His own truthful Names—All-Wise, Munificent, Just and Merciful —to be characterized by their opposites? How could He deny the true essences of all beings that indicate His Wisdom, Munificence, Justice, and Mercy, and yet rebut all things' testimony and negate the indications made by them? Can reason support the conjecture that God would impose innumerable duties upon us and our senses, and then give us only a worldly reward worth less than a hair, or that He could act absurdly and thereby contradict His true Justice and true Wisdom?

God shows Himself to be absolutely All-Wise in attaching infinite purposes and benefits to every living being (or to each of its members) and creature. Given this, would He not bestow the greatest purpose, the most significant beneficial result, the most necessary effects upon us? All of these make His Wisdom, blessings, and Mercy into what they are, and are the origin and goal of all those purposes, blessings, imprints of Mercy and beneficial results—namely, eternality, meeting with Him in the Hereafter, and everlasting bliss.

If He abandoned these, all of His acts would be pointless. He would be like a builder who built a palace consisting of stones bearing thousands of designs, corners holding thousands of adornments, and parts providing thousands of valuable tools and instruments—but forgot to cover it with a roof, so that everything therein rotted and became useless. Just as goodness comes from Absolute Goodness, and beauty comes from Absolute Beauty, a wise purpose must come from Absolute Wisdom.

Whoever studies history sees countless dead stages, places, exhibitions, and worlds, each of which is like this present world. Although different from each other in form and quality, they resemble each other in their perfect arrangement, exquisiteness, and how they display the Maker's Power and Wisdom. In those impermanent halting-places, transient arenas, and fleeting places of exhibition, we see only well-arranged works of manifest wisdom, signs of evident favoring, indications of overwhelming justice, and fruits of comprehensive mercy. Those with any perception understand that there cannot be a more perfect wisdom, gracious favoring, glorious justice, or comprehensive mercy.

Consider this: If there were no permanent abodes, elevated places, everlasting residences, eternal mansions, and no eternal residents (God's blissful servants) in the Eternal Sovereign's realm, Who does all those things and continuously changes those hostelries and their guests, we would have to reject the true essences of Wisdom, Justice, Favoring, and Mercy.

However, these four spiritual elements are as powerful and pervasive as light, air, water, and soil. Their existence, as clear as these visible elements, cannot be denied. This fleeting world and its contents cannot manifest their true essences fully. Therefore, if there were no other place wherein they could be manifested fully, we would have to deny the wisdom apparent in what we see, the favoring we observe manifested on us and all other things, the justice indicated by its signs that appear so effectively, and the mercy we witness everywhere.[27]

---

[27] There are two forms of justice, one affirmative and the other negative. The affirmative one consists in giving the right to the one who deserves it. [Except for the injustices we commit

We also would have to regard God as a foolish trickster and a pitiless tyrant, even though He is the source of all wise processes, munificent deeds, and merciful gifts that we see in the universe. Can such a reversal of the truth even be considered reasonable? Even Sophists who deny the existence of everything, including their own selves, would not readily contemplate such a proposition.

In short, the world's universal fusions of life and swift separations of death, imposing gatherings and rapid dispersions, splendid parades, performances, ceremonies, and mighty manifestations are irrec-

---

in the realm where our free wills have a part], this form of justice is clearly observed throughout the world. For, as discussed in the Third Truth, the Majestic Originator gives in definite measures and according to definite criteria everything that is asked for in the tongues of natural need and absolute necessity. In other words, He meets all the requirements of its life and existence. Therefore, this form of justice is as certain as existence and life.

The negative form of justice involves punishing the unjust, and so giving the wrong-doers their due via requital and chastisement. Even though this form is not manifested fully here, countless signs suggest its existence. For example, the blows of chastisement striking the rebellious 'Ad and Thamud peoples in the past to those of the present age show that a very exalted justice dominates the world.

oncilable with their negligible results and insignificant, temporary purposes in this fleeting world.
[If there were no Hereafter], this would mean giving a great mountain a purpose as insignificant as
a small stone. This is utterly unreasonable and pointless.

Such a large disparity between beings and those
affairs on the one hand, and the purposes they serve
in this world on the other, testifies that they basically work on behalf of the Immaterial World of
Meanings, where their true meanings will be manifested fully. They send the fruits appropriate for
them to that other world, and fix their eyes on the
Sacred Divine Names. Implanted in this world's
soil, they flourish in the World of Symbols or
Immaterial, Essential Forms.

According to our capacity, we sow and are sown
here to harvest in the Hereafter. If you look at the
aspects of things pertaining to the Divine Names
and the Hereafter, you will see that each seed (a
miracle of Power) has aims as vast as a tree, that
each blossom (a word of Divine Wis-dom) has as
many meanings as a tree's blossoms.[28] Each fruit,

_____

[28] I choose examples chiefly among seeds, flowers, and fruits
because they are the most marvelous and delicate miracles

a marvel of Divine art and a composition of Divine Mercy, has as many purposes as a tree's fruits. Serving us as foods is only one of its countless purposes.

After it fulfills that service and expresses its meaning, it dies and is "buried" in our stomachs. These transient things yield everlasting fruits in another place, where they leave permanent forms of themselves, express eternal meanings of different aspects, and constantly glorify God. We can attain true humanity by approaching things from these aspects and thereby find a way to eternity through this ephemeral world. Since this is true, all these creatures that move between life and death, that are first integrated and gathered together and then dispersed and dissolved, must serve some other purposes.

This state of affairs resembles arrangements made for imitation and representation. Brief gatherings and dispersions are arranged, at great expense, so that pictures can be taken and shown later. One

of Divine Power. Despite this, since misguided naturalists and scientists cannot "read" the subtle designs inscribed in them by the Pen of the Divine Destiny and Power, they have drowned in them and fallen into the swamp of naturalism.

reason for our brief individual and social lives is so that pictures may be taken and the results of our deeds recorded and preserved. They then will be judged in a vast place of gathering and shown in a great place of exhibition, so that all may understand that they have the potential to yield supreme happiness. The Prophet expressed this: "This world is the tillage for the Hereafter."

Since the world exists, and since Wisdom, Favoring, Mercy, and Justice prevail therein with their imprints, the Hereafter also exists. Since all worldly things are mainly turned toward that world, they are headed for it. To deny the Hereafter amounts to denying this world and its contents. Just as the appointed hour and the grave await us, so do Paradise and Hell anxiously await our arrival.

ELEVENTH TRUTH: The gate of humanity, the manifestation of the Name the Truth. Could the Almighty Truth, the only One worthy of worship, make us the most important servant to His absolute, universal Lordship, and then deny us the Eternal Abode for which we are fitted and longing? Could He make us a most comprehensive mirror in which to manifest His Names, choose us as the most thoughtful one to address, and then deny us the Eternal Abode?

Could He create us as His Power's most beautiful miracle and in the fairest form, so that we might receive His Greatest Name's manifestation as well as the greatest manifestations of all His Names, and then deny us the Eternal Abode? Could He create us as investigators equipped, more than any other creature, with measuring instruments and systems to assess and perceive the contents of Divine Mercy's treasuries, and then deny us the Eternal Abode? Could He make us more needy of His infinite bounties than all other beings, more afflicted by mortality and most desirous of eternity, and then deny us the Eternal Abode?

Could He create us as the most delicate and destitute animate being, the most wretched and susceptible to pain in worldly life but the most developed in capacity and structure, and then deny us the Eternal Abode? How could the Almighty Truth create us with all such qualities and then not send us to the Eternal Abode, for which we are fitted and longing? Could He so nullify our essence, act so totally contrary to His being the Absolute Truth, and commit an injustice that truth must condemn as ugly?

Could the Just Ruler, the Absolutely Merciful, give us the potential to bear the Supreme Trust, from which the heavens and mountains shrank, and then deny us eternal happiness? Could He enable us to measure and know, with our slight and partial measures and accomplishments, our Creator's all-encompassing Attributes, universal acts, and infinite manifestations, and then deny us eternal happiness? Could He create us as the most delicate, vulnerable, impotent, and weakest beings, task us with ordering Earth's vegetable and animal life and let us interfere with their forms of worship and glorification of God, and then deny us eternal happiness?

Could He cause us to represent His universal operations on a miniature scale, thereby declaring through us His glorious Lordship throughout the universe in word and deed, and then deny us eternal happiness? Could He prefer us over His angels and give us the rank of vicegerent, and then deny us eternal happiness?[29] Could He grant us all

---

[29] God Almighty has distinguished us with knowledge, speech, and free will. Although He allows us to act on our own

of this and then deny us eternal happiness, which is the purpose, result, and fruit of all these duties?

Consider this: He created us as the most wretched, ill-fortuned, suffering, and humiliated creature, and then gave us intelligence, a gift of His Wisdom and a most blessed and light-diffusing means of finding happiness. If He denied us eternal happiness, our intelligence would become a tool of torment. As a result, He would be acting totally contrary to His absolute Wisdom and Mercy.

Remember that we looked at an officer's identity card and register. We saw that his rank, duty, salary, instructions, and supplies caused him to exert himself for the sake of a permanent realm. Like this, as all exacting scholars and purified ones able to unveil hidden truths agree, we have been equipped with all our senses, faculties, and intel-

---

according to our free will, He wants us to rule here according to His Commandments so that the world might be integrated with other parts of the universe in peace, harmony, and tranquillity, and so that we can find the happiness in both worlds for which we long. Being vicegerent means having the authority to rule on Earth in His name, but with the responsibility of following His Commandments sent through His Prophets. (Tr.)

lectual and spiritual faculties to obtain eternal happiness.

For example, if you tell your imagination (a servant of the intellect forming conceptions) that you could live for a million years amidst royal pomp and pleasure and then undergo eternal annihilation, it would heave a deep sigh of sorrow, unless deceived by vain fancy and the carnal self.

This means that the greatest temporary worldly pleasure cannot satisfy our smallest faculty. So, as our character and disposition—desires extending to eternity, thoughts embracing all creation, and wishes felt for all varieties of eternal happiness—show, we were created for and will proceed to eternity. This world is like a waiting room for the Hereafter.

TWELFTH TRUTH: The gate of Messengership and Revelation, the manifestation of *In the Name of God, the Merciful, the Compassionate.* Could groundless fancies, wandering doubts, and illusions, all weaker than a gnat's wing, close the path to the Hereafter and the gate to Paradise? These have been opened by thousands of decisive Qur'anic verses, miraculous in 40 ways, and the noble Messenger of God, relying on the power of his almost 1,000 established miracles. This is the same Messenger whose words are affirmed by all Prophets, based on their miracles; whose claim is confirmed by saints, based on their visions and spiritual experiences and discoveries; and whose truthfulness is testified to by all purified, exacting scholars relying on their investigations.

These twelve truths show that the Resurrection is a firmly rooted truth that cannot be shaken. God Almighty established it as a requirement of His Names and Attributes, His Messenger affirms it with the strength of his miracles and the proofs of his Prophethood, the Qur'an proves it with its truths and verses, and the universe testifies to it with all its phenomena and purposeful events taking place therein. How could the Resurrection, upon which the Necessarily Existent Being and creation (except unbelievers) agree, and whose truth is as mighty and firmly rooted as mountains, be shaken by doubts feebler than a hair and satanic whisperings?

These are not the only arguments for the Resurrection, for the Qur'an, which instructs us in these Twelve Truths, points to many other aspects of this issue. And each aspect is a clear sign that our

Creator will transfer us from this transient abode to an eternal one. Also, the Divine Names requiring the Resurrection are not limited to those mentioned: All-Wise, All-Munificent, All-Compassionate, All-Just, and All-Recording and Pre-serving. In reality, all Divine Names manifested in the universe's ordering and administration require the Resurrection.

The "natural" phenomena pointing to the Resurrection are not restricted to those we have discussed. Most things in the universe have aspects and properties resembling curtains opening to the right and the left. One aspect testifies to the Maker, and the other indicates the Resurrection. For example, our creation in the fairest form demonstrates the Maker, together with the comprehensive abilities lodged in that fairest form, while our rapid decline points to the Resurrection.

If we look at the same aspect in two ways, we sometimes notice that it indicates both the Maker and the Resurrection. For example, the wise ordering and arrangement, gracious decoration, just balance and measurement, and merciful favoring seen in most things show that they proceed from the hand of the Power of an All-Wise, All-Munificent, All-Just and All-Compassionate Maker. But despite the power and infinitude of these Names and their manifestations, if we look at the brief and insignificant life of those transient beings receiving their manifestations, the Hereafter appears. Thus, in the tongue of their being and life, all things recite and lead others to recite: "I believe in God and the Last Day."

Conclusion

The preceding Twelve Truths confirm, complement, and support each other. As a single truth, they demonstrate the desired result. Can any doubt penetrate those twelve firm walls, each like steel or diamonds, and shake the belief in the Resurrection housed within them?

Your creation and your resurrection are as but a single soul (31:28) means that creating and resurrecting humanity or a single person are equally easy for the Divine Power. In *Nukta* (Point), I elaborated this truth. Here, I will summarize it and present various comparisons.[30] For example, if the sun had free will and could manifest itself however it wished, as a light-giving object it could do

---

[30] This treatise is included in Said Nursi's *Mathnawi Nuriya*, which is available in English as *Epitomes of Light*. (Tr.)

so with the same ease in innumerable transparent objects or in one particle.[31] Being transparent, the tiniest transparent thing equals the ocean's surface in containing the sun's image. By virtue of orderliness and its interrelated parts, a child can steer a battleship as easily as a toy boat. By virtue of obedience, a commander can order an army to move with the same "March!" issued to one soldier.

Imagine a balance so sensitive that it can weigh two walnuts, and so large that it can weigh two suns. If two walnuts or suns of equal weight were placed in these pans, the resulting equilibrium, the same power that lifts one walnut to the heavens and lowers the other to the ground, would move the suns with the same ease.

In this lowly, imperfect, and transient World of Contingency, and by virtue of such qualities as luminosity, transparency, orderliness and interrelatedness, obedience and balance (or equilibrium), all things become equal, and numerous things appear as equal to one thing. Given this, and by virtue of the luminous manifestations of the Absolutely

---

[31] In fact, the sun is manifested with the same ease in everything, without any one hindering any other.

Powerful One's essential, infinite, and utterly perfect Power; the transparency of the inner dimension of things; the exact universal order dictated by Divine Wisdom and Destiny; the perfect obedience of things to His command of creation; and because the existence or non-existence of all things is equally possible, little and much, small and great are equal in respect to His Power. And so He will resurrect us with one trumpet blast, as if we were one person.

Furthermore, a thing's degrees of strength and weakness are determined by the intervention of its opposite. Degrees of heat are determined by cold's intervention, degrees of beauty by ugliness' intervention, and degrees of illumination by darkness' intervention. But if a quality or property is essential to something, that is, if it originates directly from itself and is almost identical with itself, its opposite cannot intervene in it. If its opposite could intervene, this would mean that opposites of the same qualities would have to be united in a single thing—something clearly impossible.

The Absolutely Powerful One's Power is essential to His Divine Essence, originates from It directly, and is almost identical with It. Given this, and that It is also absolutely perfect, It cannot have an opposite to intervene in It. Hence the Lord of Majesty creates spring as easily as He creates a flower, and will resurrect and assemble humanity with the same ease as He resurrects one person. If material causes had to create just one flower, on the other hand, they would have to be able to create an entire spring.

All that we have explained so far is derived from the radiation of the Wise Qur'an. So, let's listen to more of what it has to say:

> For God is the final, conclusive argument. (6:149)

> Look upon the signs and imprints of God's Mercy, how He revives the soil after its death. He it is Who will revive the dead [in the same way]. He is powerful over all things. (30:50)

> [Humanity] coins for Us a similitude, and forgets his own creation, saying: "Who will revive those bones when they have rotted away?" Say: "The One Who first produced them will revive them. He is Knower of every creation." (36:78-79)

> O humanity, fear your Lord. The quaking of the Hour is a mighty thing. The day you see it, every suckling woman shall forget her suckling-babe, and every pregnant one shall drop her burden. You shall see

humanity as drunk, yet they are not drunk. Dreadful will be the doom of God. (22:1-2)

God, there is no god but He. Surely He will gather you all to a Day of Judgment about which there is no doubt. Who is more true than God in the words [He speaks] and the news [He gives]? (4:87)

The pious, purified will be in bliss and blessings. The wicked will be in blazing Fire. (82:13-14)

When Earth is shaken with its [final and terrible] earthquake and throws up its burdens, and humanity asks: "What is the matter with it?" That day it will proclaim its tidings because Your Lord has inspired it. That day humanity will come forth in scattered groups to be shown their deeds. Whoever does an atom's weight of good shall see it, whoever does an atom's weight of evil shall see it. (99:1-8)

The noise and clamor! What is the noise and clamor? Would that you knew what the noise and clamor is! The day whereon humanity will be like moths scattered about, and the mountains will be like carded wool. Then those whose scales are heavy [in good deeds] will be in a pleasing life. But those whose scales are light, shall plunge in the womb of a [bottomless] Pit. What will convey to you what that is like? A raging Fire! (101:1-11)

To God belongs the unseen of the heavens and Earth. The affair of the Hour is as the twinkling of an eye, or even quicker. God is powerful over all things. (16:77)

Listening to these and other similar verses, we should say: "We so believe and affirm."

I believe in God, His angels, books, Messengers, the Last Day, and Destiny in that whatever comes as good or evil [is recorded in His Knowledge and created by Him]. Resurrection is true, Paradise is true, the Fire is true, intercession [on the Last Day] is true, and Munkar and Nakir are true.[32] God will resurrect those in the graves. I bear witness that there is no god but God, and I bear witness that Muhammad is the Messenger of God.

O God, bestow blessings on the most graceful, noble and dignified, perfect and beautiful fruit of Your Mercy, which has blossomed throughout the universe like a blessed tree; on him whom You sent as a mercy for all worlds, and as a means for us to attain to the most adorned, fairest, brightest, and most exalted fruit of that "tree" extending into the Hereafter, that is, into Paradise. O God, save us and our parents from the Fire, and take us and our parents into Paradise with the purified, pious ones, for the sake of Your chosen Prophet. Amen.

---

[32] Munkar and Nakir are the two angels who interrogate the dead about their beliefs and deeds in this world. (Ed.)

If you are studying this treatise with an open mind, do not ask: "Why can't I immediately understand this Tenth Word in all its details?" Do not become bored if you cannot understand it right away. Even such a master of philosophy as Ibn Sina judged that the Resurrection could not be understood through rational criteria. As it is beyond human reason, we must believe in it.

Also, almost all scholars of Islam consider it one of the revealed truths requiring belief and one that cannot be established through reason. Therefore, it is difficult for human reason to grasp such a profound and exalted issue. Thanks to the Merciful Creator's Mercy and the Wise Qur'an's radiation, I hope that this Tenth Word, if studied carefully and repeatedly, will convince your reason of the Resurrection's truth and help secure belief in it.

One difficulty that human reason encounters here is that since the Resurrection and Great Gathering will occur through the manifestation of God's Greatest Name, this event can be established rationally only by demonstrating His acts through His Greatest Name's manifestation and the universal manifestations of other Names, as if proving the coming of next spring. We followed this approach in this Word.

Addendum

In the Name of God,
the Merciful, the Compassionate.

So glory be to God, when you enter the night and when you enter the morning. To Him be praise in the heavens and on Earth, and when the day begins to decline, and at the time of noon. He brings out the living from the dead, and brings out the dead from the living, and He gives life to the soil after it is dead: and in this way you [also] will be brought out [from the dead]. Among His signs is this: He created you from soil, and then—behold, you are people scattered [far and wide]! And among His signs is this: He created for you mates from among yourselves, that you may live in restfulness with them, and He has put love and mercy between you. Surely in that are signs for those who reflect. And among His signs is the creation of the heavens and Earth, and the variations in your languages and your colors. Surely in that are signs for those who know. And among His signs is the sleep that you take by night and by day, and your quest for livelihood out of His bounty. Surely in that are signs for those who pay heed. And among His signs, He shows you the lightning in a way to give you both fear and hope [at the same time], and He sends down rain from the

> sky and with it gives life to Earth after it is dead.
> Surely in that are signs for those who reason. And
> among His signs is this: Heaven and Earth stand
> [firm] by His Command: then when He calls you,
> by a single call, from Earth—behold: you [straight-
> away] come forth. To Him belongs every being that
> is in the heavens and on Earth: all are obedient to
> Him. It is He Who produces creation, then reproduces
> it; and for Him it is most easy. To Him belongs the
> highest similitude [that we can think of and coin
> concerning Him] in the heavens and Earth. He is
> the Mighty, the All-Wise. (30:17-27)

These sublime, God-revealed verses, high and
sacred proofs of the Resurrection's reality, establish one pole of the belief. From those proofs, one
significant argument is here set forth. It was a subtle instance of Divine grace that, at the end of
Muhakemat (Reasonings), which I wrote about 30
years ago to set down the principles of Qur'anic
commentary, came the words: "Second Aim: Two
verses of the Qur'an referring to the Resurrection
to be expounded and made clear." And there it
stopped.

Praise and thanks as numerous as the proofs of
my Merciful Lord and the evidences for the
Resurrection that, 30 years later on, I have been
enabled to resume that task. About 9 or 10 years ago,

God granted to me the Tenth and Twenty-ninth Words, two works containing numerous strong proofs and interpretations of the Divine Decree—*Look upon the signs and imprints of God's Mercy, how He revives the soil after its death. Surely He will revive the dead [in the same way], and He is powerful over all things*—the first of the two verses in question.

The Tenth and Twenty-ninth Words silenced those who denied the Resurrection. Now, a decade or so later, He has granted to me the interpretation of the second of those supreme verses, unassailable fortresses of belief in the Resurrection. That interpretation is related here.

Part one: Two points

[This introduction consists of two points that briefly expound one of the many spiritual benefits of belief in the Resurrection and one of its vital comprehensive results. They also show how that belief is essential for human life, particularly social life, and summarize one of its many comprehensive proofs. Also included is an explanation of how evident and indubitable a matter is belief in the Resurrection.]

FIRST POINT: We will relate only four of the many arguments for belief in the Hereafter as the very basis and bedrock of human social and individual life, and the foundation of all happiness and achievement.

FIRST ARGUMENT: Children are one-fourth of humanity. They cannot endure death, which must seem to them an awful tragedy, except via the idea of Paradise, which spiritually strengthens their weak, fragile natures. It gives them the hope to live joyfully, despite the vulnerability of their nature, which can so readily burst into tears.

Keeping Paradise in mind, they may say: "My little sister or friend has died and become a bird in Paradise. She is playing there and enjoying a better life." If they could not do this, their awareness of the deaths of those around them would overwhelm them; crush their powers of resistance and inner strength; cause their eyes and all inner faculties, heart, mind, and spirit to weep; and destroy them or transform them into distraught and crazed animals.

SECOND ARGUMENT: The elderly make up another one-fourth of humanity. They can endure death only by believing in the afterlife, which consoles them somewhat for the imminent extinction of this life to which they are so attached, for their exclusion from their lovely world. The hope of eternal life allows them to counter the pain and despair arising from the anticipation of death and separation, despite their fragile temperament and spirit. Without such a hope, our venerable elders who are so worthy of respect, our aged parents who need a serene and steady heart, would become so distraught in spirit and distressed at heart that their world would seem to be a dark prison, their lives a heavy burden of torment.

THIRD ARGUMENT: Young people are the mainspring and foundation of social life. Only the thought of Hell enables them to control the stormy energy of feelings and passions, their tempestuous spirits, from destructiveness and oppression by diverting them into serving the collective interest. Without this fear, and drunk on youth's energy of youth, they would follow the principle of "might makes right" and give free rein to their passions. This would turn the world into a hell for the weak and powerless, and lower human life to the level of beasts.

FOURTH ARGUMENT: The family is the inclusive core of our worldly life, our most fundamental resource, and the paradise, home, and castle of our worldly happiness. Each person's home is his or her own miniature world. The vitality and happiness of our homes and families depend upon sincere and devoted respect, true kindness, and self-denying compassion. All of this, in turn, depends upon eternal friendship and companionship, an immortal bond, as well as the belief that feelings between parents and children, brothers and sisters, and husbands and wives will be everlasting.

For example, a man can say: "My wife will be my eternal companion in an eternal world. Even if she is now old and not as beautiful as before, her eternal beauty will show itself in the Hereafter. For the sake of that companionship in eternity, I sacrifice and show her compassion in this world." Thus he can regard his aged wife with love, care, and compassion, as if she were a gorgeous houri. A companionship that ends in permanent separation after a few hours of bodily togetherness can only be slight, transient, and insecure. It would produce only a superficial love and respect based on physical charm and sexual instinct. Other interests and powerful emotions eventually would arise and, defeating that respect and concern, turn a worldly paradise into a worldly hell.

One of this belief's many benefits therefore relates to our social life. If the related aspects and benefits are deduced via analogy with these four, it will be clear that the Resurrection's reality and truth is as certain as our own existence and universal need. It will be even more evident than the argument that food must exist because our stomachs require it.

If the Resurrection's reality and truth, and all the consequences thereof, are subtracted from the human state, the meaning of being human—so exalted, vital, and important within creation—is lowered to that of a carcass fed upon by microbes. Let those concerned with humanity's orderly life, morals, and society focus on this matter. If the Resurrection is denied, with what will they fill the resulting void and cure the deep wounds?

SECOND POINT: We set out, in a compressed and succinct form, the support offered by the other pillars of belief. All miracles affirming Muhammad as Messenger, all proofs of his Prophethood, and all evidence of his truthfulness bear witness to and establish the Resurrection's reality and truth. After the Unity of God Almighty, that exalted man spent his life focused on the Resurrection. Indeed, the miracles and proofs attesting to all Prophets, and urging humanity to attest to them, bear witness to the same truth. Similarly, the requirement for Muslims to believe in His Messengers is necessarily followed by belief in His Books, which also bear witness to this truth.

All miracles, proofs, and truths establishing the Qur'an's truth likewise establish and prove the Resurrection's reality and truth. About one-third of the Qur'an deals with the Hereafter, most of its short *sura*s begin with powerful verses evoking it, and it proclaims this truth explicitly or implicitly in hundreds of verses, thereby proving it. For example:

> When the sun is folded up. (81:1)
>
> O humanity, fear your Lord; the quaking of the Hour is a mighty thing. (22:1)
>
> When Earth is shaken. (99:1)
>
> When the heavens are torn asunder. (82:1)
>
> When the heavens are torn apart. (84:1)

Whereof do they question each other? (78:1)

Has the story of the overwhelming event reached you? (88:1)

Just as the initial verses of about 20 *sura*s state that the Resurrection's truth is most important and essential for humanity, many other verses affirm and provide other evidence of the same truth. How can you even consider not believing in the Resurrection? Such a belief is made as clear as the sun by the additional uncountable testimonies and claims in a Book that yields the fruit of all scientific and cosmic truths contained in the Islamic sciences, even though one reference in one verse would suffice. Do you also deny the existence of the sun or the universe?

A sovereign sometimes sends his army into battle merely to prove the truth of one of his statements. Is it, then, even conceivable to deny the truth of that most solemn and proud Sovereign's innumerable words, promises, and threats? One indication from the Glorious Sovereign suffices to prove the Resurrection's truth, especially since His Qur'an has ruled, administered, and educated countless spirits, intellects, hearts and souls according to perfect righteousness and truth for more than 13 centuries. Having proved and demonstrated this truth with thousands of explicit proofs, what else can we say than that those who continue to deny this truth are worthy of and deserve punishment in Hellfire?

Similarly, all Divine Pages and Sacred Books other than the Qur'an, each of which was addressed to a specific age and time, accept it. Thus it is logical for the Qur'an, the Book addressed to the future and all ages, to expound upon it in such detail and with such explicit arguments. Even their brief and sometimes allusive explanations affirm it so powerfully that they constitute a thousandfold signature of what is revealed in the Qur'an.

We include an argument drawn from the *Treatise on Supplication*. This brief argument, including the testimony of belief in the Last Day by the other pillars of belief, mainly belief in God's Messengers and Books, is forceful and may suffice to end all doubt. In this supplication, we say:

> O Compassionate Lord. Through the noble Messenger's teaching and the Wise Qur'an's instruction, I have understood that all Divine Books and Prophets, primarily the Qur'an and Your noble Messenger, assert and testify that the manifestations

of all Your Names of Majesty and Grace, the exemplary radiations of which are witnessed throughout the universe, will continue to be manifested in eternity in a more splendid way; that Your bounties and blessings, the merciful manifestations and specimens of which are observed in this world, will persist in a more brilliant fashion in the Abode of Eternal Bliss; and that those who are fond of them and who discern them in this brief worldly life with pleasure and seek them in love will accompany them eternally in the Hereafter.

Moreover all Prophets, led by Your noble Messenger, who relied on their hundreds of manifest miracles and evident signs of their truthfulness as well as the decisive Divine verses they brought, are masters of all illustrious and illuminated "spirits"; all saints who are leaders of all illumined "hearts"; and all truthful and purified scholars who are sources inspiring all keen, enlightened intellects—they give humanity the good tidings of eternal happiness, and proclaim and testify with firm belief that there is Hellfire for the misguided and Paradise for the truly guided.

They do this on the basis of the promises and threats You have reiterated in all Heavenly Pages and Sacred Books; on all Your sacred Attributes such as Power, Mercy, Favoring, Wisdom, Majesty, and Grace, all of which require the Resurrection; on Your Majesty's dignity and might and Your Lordship's sovereignty; and on their innumerable visions and observations, as well as their belief and conviction in the degree of certainty coming from true knowledge and direct observation, that convey to us the traces and effects of the Hereafter.

O All-Powerful and All-Wise One. O All-Merciful, All-Compassionate. O All-Munificent, Truthful in His Promises! O Possessor of Splendor, Grandeur, and Majesty, All-Overwhelming One. You are far exalted above causing so many of Your sincere friends to appear as liars, or rendering false the testimony of so many of Your Names and Attributes, or rebutting and denying the reality of what is required by Your Lordship's Sovereignty, or refusing the innumerable prayers and petitions for the Hereafter of Your innumerable servants whom You love and who seek Your love with belief in You and obedience to You, or supporting the denial of the Resurrection made by the misguided who insult Your Glory and Majesty with their rebellious unbelief and their belying Your promises, and who transgress Your Lordship's Majesty.

We proclaim to the utmost degree the transcendence and sanctity of Your infinite Justice, Beauty, and Mercy, as well as their exaltation above such boundless injustice and abomination. We believe with all our power to believe in the reality and truth of what has been told with utmost certainty by innumerable truthful Messengers, all Prophets, purified scholars, and saints—all of them are Heralds of Your Sovereignty—about the treasuries of Your eternal Mercy, the riches of Your Bounty to be veiled in the everlasting realm, and the wonderful, mirac-

ulous manifestations of Your Beautiful Names that
will fully appear in the Abode of Happiness. Their
indications are true and correct, and their prophesy-
ing is truthful. They teach Your servants, by Your
command and in accordance with truth, that the
greatest ray to emerge from the Name "Truth"—
which is the origin, sun, and protector of all truths—
is the sublime truth of the Resurrection. They believe
in this and teach it as the essence of truth.

O Lord, for the sake of their instruction and teach-
ing, grant to us and our brothers and sisters perfect-
ed belief and a fair ending to our life, and that we
may have some share of their intercession. Amen.

All arguments and evidences establishing the
Qur'an's truth, and that of all Divine Books, as well as
the miracles and proofs establishing the Prophethood
of the beloved of God—Prophet Muhammad—and
of all Prophets, point to the Hereafter's reality. This
reality dominates the truth affirmed by the Books
and the Messengers.

Similarly, most arguments and evidences for the
Necessarily Existent Being's Existence and Unity
implicitly affirm the existence and opening out
of the Abode of Happiness, the Realm of Eternity
where God's Lordship and Divinity will be fully
shown. The Necessarily Existent Being's existence

requires the Hereafter's existence, as do all of His Attributes, most of His Names, and His essential Qualities (e.g., Lordship, Divinity, Grace, Wisdom, and Justice). These require an eternal realm, as the Resurrection is required for dispensing just punishment and reward.

An eternally existent God requires a Hereafter that is the everlasting pivot of His Divine Sovereignty. We can see that a most magnificent, purposively wise, and caring absolute Lordship exists throughout the universe and animate creation. Given this, there must be an eternal realm of happiness to which admission is granted, so that His Magnificence is not extinguished, His Wisdom not turned into pointlessness, and His Caring not destroyed by betrayal.

These visible and infinite bounties, blessings, kindnesses, and instances of generosity and mercy show that a Merciful and Compassionate Being exists beyond the veil of the Unseen. Given this, there must be an eternal life in an eternal world, for only that which will show that His Divine bounties do not mock, His blessings do not deceive, His favoring does not create enmity, His mercy does not torment, and His generosity does not betray. In addition, eternity and ceaselessness make all bounties and blessings assume their true and perfect forms.

Each spring we see a Pen of Power tirelessly inscribe uncountable interleaved books on the narrow page of Earth. Not one of them contains an error. The Owner of that Pen has promised repeatedly: "I shall write and have you read a beautiful, imperishable book in a place far more spacious than this, and in a fashion far easier than this cramped and intermingled book of spring that is written on such a narrow page." He mentions this book in all of His decrees. Its origin has been written already, and will be set down in writing with all its marginalia on the Day of Resurrection.

Earth has a special importance: It is the universe's heart, center, choice, core, ultimate end, and very reason for its creation. It enjoys this status because of the multiplicity of its inhabitants and because it is the abode, origin, workshop, and place of display and resurrection of countless constantly changing forms. Despite its small size, the Qur'an describes Earth as equivalent to the vast heavens. Thus we read in the Heavenly Books: *the Lord of the heavens and Earth.*

Humanity also is of supreme importance. We are dominant throughout Earth. We have dominion over most of its creatures, subordinate and gather around ourselves almost all animate beings, and order, display, and ornament created objects according to our need and desire. We catalogue and classify everything in all its wonderful variety, each species in its own place, and in such a way that all people and jinn gaze at it, all dwellers of the heavens and the universe regard it with appreciation, and even the Lord of the universe bestows His appreciative glance upon it.

As we have a very high value and thus importance, our art and science show that we are the reason for the universe's creation. Our great consequence and status as creation's supreme fruit is in our serving as God's vicegerents. Since we demonstrate and arrange the Maker's miraculous works here, we are given a respite and our punishment is postponed, despite our rebellion and disbelief. And, due to the services we perform, we are granted a temporary stay and the Almighty's assistance.

Despite being endowed with such qualities, we nevertheless are extremely weak and impotent when it comes to fulfilling the demands of our nature and disposition. And yet a most powerful, wise, and caring Ruler provides for us in a way altogether beyond our power and will. He makes the planet a storehouse stocked with every kind of mineral and food we need and with all the merchandise we desire. Thus does the Ruler take care of and nurture us and grant our wishes.

The Lord thus possesses these qualities. He loves us and makes Himself our beloved. He is Eternal and has eternal worlds. He does all things with justice and wisdom. But this Exalted Ruler's magnificent splendor and eternality cannot be encompassed within the transient life of this fleeting, temporary world. Furthermore, the sheer enormity of human injustice and rebellion, which is hostile to and contradicts the universe's just balance and harmonious beauty, not to mention its members' betrayal, denial, and unbelief toward their Benefactor and Provider —all of these go unpunished in this world. The cruel and the treacherous live easily, while the oppressed and downcast live in wretchedness.

But the whole nature and being of Absolute Justice, signs of which are seen throughout the universe, are totally at odds and irreconcilable with the idea that the cruel and treacherous—who die just like the oppressed and the desperate—should never be resurrected [to account for their cruelty in a supreme tribunal].

The Master of all that is has chosen this world and given to it a high rank and significance. Out of all its creatures, He has given rank and significance to humanity. In the same way, He has chosen Prophets, saints, and purified scholars as His friends and objects of His address, for they show that they are truly human by conforming to the purposes of the Lord of creation. They make themselves beloved of their Maker through belief and submission, and He ennobles them with miracles and Divine support and chastises their opponents with blows from heaven.

From these people, He has chosen their leader and fulcrum: Muhammad. He enlightened him and, by his light, has illumined for centuries one-fifth of humanity. It is as if creation were created for his sake, for all of its high purposes become manifest through him, his religion, and the Qur'an he brought. Although he deserved and was worthy to receive an infinite reward for the infinite value of the services he rendered, which usually would take thousands of years to perform, he was granted a brief life of 63 years spent in hardship and struggle. How could we believe that he would not be resurrected, together with all his peers—the other Prophets—and Companions? Or that he should not, even now, be alive in the spirit? Or that they should die and disappear into eternal extinction?

The universe and the truth on which it is based demand his being again, demand his life from the Owner of all that is. his life from the Owner of all that is. We have established in the *Risale-i Nur* that the universe is a Single Being's handicraft, and that that Being's Oneness and Unity, which give rise to all His perfections, cause creation to obey Him absolutely. By means of a new life, that of the Hereafter, those perfections remain defect-free[33]; His Absolute Justice is not deformed into absolute treachery; or His universal Wisdom into foolish pointlessness; or His all-inclusive Mercy into frivolous tormenting; or His exalted Power confounded with impotence.

---

[33] The Divine perfections will be manifested without veil in this realm. The defects referred to are such things as injustice, hardship, cruelty, and all disparities that humanity, having free will, suffers and causes others to suffer. (Ed.)

The Resurrection will occur. These points, along with hundreds of others derived from belief in God, prove this. Only after the abodes of reward and punishment open their gates will Earth's significance and centrality, and our true significance and value, be truly accomplished. Then, the Wise Ruler's Justice, Wisdom, Mercy, and Sovereignty, Who is the Creator and Lord of our planet and of us, will be manifested eternally with all their perfection.

All true friends and ardent lovers of the Eternal Lord will be delivered from eternal annihilation, and the nearest and dearest of them will be rewarded for the sacred services with which He gratified the world. Then the Eternal Sovereign's perfections will affirm themselves to be without defect, His Power without incompetency, and His Justice without oppressiveness. In sum, the Hereafter exists because God exists.

The articles of faith explained above bear witness to the Resurrection, along with all the evidences testifying to their truth. The remaining two articles of faith—belief in His angels and in Destiny, whatever good or evil happens to us being included in it and created by God Almighty —require the

Resurrection and bear witness to the World of Eternity.

All arguments, testimonies, and conversations held with them, which prove that angels exist and serve God, also attest indirectly to the existence of the World of Spirits, the Unseen, the Hereafter, the Abode of Bliss that in the future will be peopled by humanity and jinn, and to Paradise and Hell. Angels perceive and enter those worlds. All angels nearest to the Divine Throne and who communicate with humanity, such as Gabriel, report their existence and travels therein. Just as we accept America's existence (which we have never actually seen) from the reports of returning travelers, so do we believe in the existence of the Realm of Eternity, the Hereafter, Paradise and Hell, from the angels' reports, which have the authority of numerous undisputed narrations.

All arguments contained in The Twenty-sixth Word (about Divine Decree and Destiny), which establish that article of faith, attest indirectly to the Resurrection, to the publishing in another world of our recorded deeds (in this world), and their weighing in the Supreme Balance. The events in the existence of all things are impressed before our eyes and recorded. The life history of every animate being is inscribed in its memory, its seed, and other tablet-like forms; the deeds of every being endowed with spirit, especially humanity, are registered on preserved tablets.

Such an all-embracing Decree, wise and purposive ordaining, detailed and minutely exact recording and inscribing exists only to enable the giving of a permanent reward or punishment at the Supreme Judgment after a universal tribunal. If this were not so, such a comprehensive, meticulous recording and registering would have no purpose or meaning, and would be contrary to sense and reality. Moreover, if there were no Resurrection, all exactly established meanings inscribed by the Pen of Divine Destiny in the Book of the Universe would be annihilated. This would be tantamount to denying the universe's existence.

In short, then, the five articles of faith and their proofs point to and require, bear witness to and necessitate, the Resurrection and that the Realm of the Hereafter be opened out. Due to the imposing foundations and unshakable arguments for it, which are worthy of that truth's sublimity, about one-third the Qur'an is devoted to it. The Qur'an makes it the bedrock of all of its truths, and constructs everything on its basis.

Part two

> Look upon the signs and imprints of God's Mercy, how He revives Earth after its death. Surely He it is Who will revive the dead [in the same way], and He is powerful over all things. (30:50)

This verse contains nine convincing arguments for the Resurrection. The first, concerning life and will be expounded upon below, is very clear and pointed to in:

> Glory be to God, when you enter evening and when you enter morning. All praise is to Him in the heavens and on Earth and at nightfall and when you enter noon. He brings forth the living from the dead and the dead from the living, and revives Earth after its death. So you will be brought forth. (30:17-19)

Life has a connection with the six articles of faith and establishes them by a series of indications of their truth. Life is the most important consequence of, and the most substantial reason for, the universe's creation. Life, that noble reality, cannot be restricted to this fleeting, transient, defective, and painful world. Rather, the tree of life's fruit, the purpose and result worthy of being such a fruit, is the Hereafter's eternal life—life in the realm where even stones, trees, and soil will be animate.

If this were not so, the tree of life, so abundantly adorned with significant means, could yield no fruit, benefit, or truth worthy of animate beings, and especially not for us. Humanity, the most important and elevated creature as regards happiness in the worldly life, would fall below a sparrow, even though the sparrow is far inferior in substance and faculties, and become the least fortunate and most humiliated of all poor creatures.

Similarly intelligence, our most precious possession, would wound our hearts by always reflecting upon past hardships and future fears. It would mix one part of pleasure with nine parts of hardship and grief, and so become a means of disaster to human life. As this cannot be, life here is a decisive argument for belief in the Hereafter. It parades before our eyes each spring in the form of infinite specimens being revived (an image of the Resurrection).

Could an All-Powerful Agent Who promptly supplies and provides, with wisdom, care and mercy, everything needed by your life, body, garden, and homeland; Who hears and answers even your stomach's private, particular petition for sustenance by providing so many delicious foods—is it conceivable that such a Being should be unaware of you or deaf to you, that He should not provide you with the means of eternal life, the highest purpose of being human?

How could He not establish eternal life and create Paradise to answer our greatest, most significant, worthy and universal prayer for eternity? How could He not hear and grant our universal and insistent prayer, given that we are His most important creature and vicegerent, a prayer that resounds throughout the heavens and Earth, while He does so for our stomachs? Could He cause His perfect Wisdom and infinite Mercy to be denied?

He hears the tiniest being's innermost voice, cures its injury, relieves its complaint, nourishes it with the utmost care and consideration, and causes other creatures to serve it. Given this, how could He not hear the thunderous cry of the greatest, most valued and subtle form of life, or ignore its powerful prayer and plea for eternity? Doing so would be like lavishly equipping a soldier and neglecting a large obedient army, seeing a speck and over-looking the sun, hearing a whirring fly and not the roaring thunder.

The All-Powerful and All-Wise Being has infinite Mercy, Love, and Caring. He loves His own artistry, causes Himself to be loved, and greatly loves those who love Him. Could such a Being use permanent death and non-existence to annihilate the spirit (life's essence and core) that greatly loves Him, is itself lovable, and that by its nature worships Him as its Maker? Would He offend and rebuff it forever or injure its sentiments, thereby denying and causing others to deny His Mercy's meaning and His Love's light? An absolute Beauty that makes creation beautiful by showing itself, and an absolute Mercy that enables all creatures to rejoice, are exalted and far above such infinite ugliness and lack of pity.

In sum, people who understand life's purpose and so do not waste their lives will become reflective displays of eternal Paradise. All transparent objects on Earth's surface, such as brilliant bubbles catching and then reflecting flashes of the sun's light, hold up mirrors to it and contain its image. Such images show that each flash of light is the reflected manifestation of the one, supreme sun.

With their many and diverse tongues, they mention the sun and point toward it with their "fingers" of light.

In a like manner, through the supreme manifestation of the Name "Giver of Life" of the Ever-Living and Self-Subsistent Being, all animate beings here shine back life through God's Power. They then disappear behind the veil of the Unseen (die), demonstrating the Ever-Living One's ever-living quality. They die to make room for new arrivals, who stream here in a continual series of testimonies to and indications of the Ever-Living and Self-Subsistent Being's Life and Necessary Existence.

Similarly, all arguments attesting to Divine Knowledge, traces of which are visible in the ordering of all beings; all evidence establishing the existence of a Power controlling the universe; all proofs pointing to a Will directing the universe's arrangement and administering; all signs and miracles attesting to the Prophets' Messengership, the means by which He addresses His creation and reveals His commands; and the indications bearing witness to Divinity's seven Attributes[34]—all of these

---

[34] God has three kinds of Attributes: the Essential Attributes of the "Essence," Affirmative Attributes, and Negative Attributes.

point and testify to the Ever-Living and Self-Subsistent Being's life. If a creature can see, it must have life; if it can hear, it must be able to speak.

Similarly, such Attributes whose existence is established and self-evident by their traces throughout the universe (e.g., Absolute Power, All-Embracing Will, and Comprehensive Knowledge) bear witness, together with all their proofs, to the Ever-Living and Self-Subsistent Being's Life and Necessary Existence. They testify to His everlast-

---

His Affirmative Attributes refer to the assertion of His absolute Unity; His Negative Attributes refer to the negation of limitation and compositeness. The Essential Attributes of the Essence are Existence, Having no beginning, Permanence, Dissimilarity to the Created and Self-Subsistence. The Affirmative Attributes, pointed to in the text above, are Life, Knowledge, Power, Will, Speech, Seeing, Hearing, and, according to some theologians, Creation. The Negative Attributes can be explained as follows: God cannot be described by any physical or anthropomorphic terms. He does not consist of body, color, and size. No person or thing can see Him, imagine, or conceive Him. He cannot be presented in the terms of substance or contingency of matter or form, localized in any part of space, confined to any part of time, or aligned and counted with any being. Nothing can be co-existent or co-extensive with Him. He never begets nor is begotten. And so on. (Tr.)

ing Life, one shadow of which suffices to light the universe, one manifestation of which suffices to give life to the Hereafter and all its component particles.

His Attribute of Life is linked to belief in angels and argues for it indirectly. Life is the universe's most important purpose. Animate beings make up the most diversely spread type of creation, and its kinds and species are multiplied on account of their worth. They continually enliven this world with their coming and going in caravans. Earth, stocked with so many living species, is continually emptied and restocked as diverse species are renewed, varied, and increased.

Even its vilest and most rotten substances give life to so many living things that they hosts swarms of microscopic organisms. Intelligence and consciousness (life's distilled essence) and spirit (life's subtle and stable substance) exist everywhere on Earth in the greatest multiplicity, as if this planet were teeming and bursting with the joy of life, intellect, consciousness, and spirit.

Given this, it seems impossible that the more subtle and lustrous heavenly bodies, all of which are far more significant in dimension than Earth, should be inanimate and entirely without life, move-ment, or voice. Thus there must be live and con-scious beings enlivening the skies, suns, and stars. They must be giving the heavenly realm their vital-ity and so possessing them of the purpose for which the heavens were created, and receiving address-es from the Glorious One. These creatures are angels.

Similarly, life's meaning and essential nature establishes belief in the Prophets. The universe was created for the sake of life, and life is one of the supreme manifestations of the Living, Self-Subsistent, and Eternal One, and one of His most perfect designs and most beautiful arts. God's eter-nal life is declared by sending Messengers and revealed Books. Without these, His being eternal would remain unknown. Just as we are considered alive when we speak, the Being from behind the Unseen (veiled by the visible universe) speaks and sends out His commands and prohibitions via Prophets and revealed Books.

The presence of life in the universe testifies to the Living and Eternal One's Necessary Exis-tence, and indicates and indirectly confirms the sending of Messengers and the revelation of Scriptures, for both are rays and manifestations of that Eternal

Life. In particular, Muhammad's Prophethood and the Qur'anic revelation, both the very spirit and intellect of life, are established as irrefutably as life's very existence.

Life is the extract distilled from the universe. Sentience (consciousness and feeling) is the extract distilled from life, intellect is the extract distilled from sentience, and spirit is life's pure and unalloyed substance, its stable and independent essence. The Prophet's physical and spiritual life is the purest extract, distilled from the universe's life and meaning; His Messengership is the pure and distilled essence of the universe's sentience, consciousness, and intellect. His life and accomplishments, in both their physical and immaterial, spiritual aspects, have proved themselves to be the true essence of the universe's life, and his Messengership is the true light and essence of the universe's consciousness. As its living and enlivening truths bear witness, the Qur'an is the spirit of the universe's life and the intellect of its consciousness.

If his Messengership's light disappeared from the universe, the latter would die. If the Qur'an were to forsake the universe, the universe would lose its sanity, and Earth would lose its reason. Dizzy and uncomprehending, it would collide with another planet and cause its own destruction.

Life also is linked to belief in Divine Destiny and establishes it indirectly. Life is the visible world's light, pervading and dominating it. It is the result and goal of existence, the most inclusive mirror to the universe's Creator, the most perfect sample and index of His activity as Lord, and a kind of program. The meaning of life requires that the Unseen world's creatures, in the past and future, be disposed to conform to some order, regularity, and other rules or commands.

Some of these beings are visible, each in its individual form and character, such as the Almighty Creator has decreed for them to govern their lives. For example, a tree's original seed and root, as well as seeds contained in its life's outcome (fruit), each have the same degree of life as the entire tree. Indeed, they carry within themselves laws of life that are more subtle than those of the tree. The seeds and roots left last autumn for the present spring, as well as the seeds and roots that will be left to subsequent springs, all bear life's visible imprint no less than the spring does, and are subject to its laws.

All branches and twigs of the cosmic tree likewise have a past and a future. They constitute a chain of past and future stages and circumstances. The multiple life stages of all species and all of their individual members, which exist in Divine Knowledge, form a chain of being in meaning or knowledge. Like the external (material) existence of things, their existence in knowledge or meaning also bears an aspect or manifestation of life. All the life stages of a living being, as well as whatever happens to it during its life, are the "materialized" duplication of its life in Divine Knowl-edge. What we call Destiny is, in one respect, a title of that Knowledge.

The World of Spirits, a kind of Unseen world, is full of spirits that constitute life's essence and substances and thus requires that past and future (another kind of Unseen world or its second form) receive its manifestation.[35]

---

[35] The original word corresponding to what we translate as "the Unseen" or "the world of the Unseen" is *ghayb*: that which we cannot penetrate with our five senses, or is invisible and unknown to us until we somehow acquire knowledge of it. Like the World of Spirits that we cannot see, and the nature of which we cannot know through our senses, past and future are also unknown to us unless we somehow obtain

In addition, the perfect orderliness and meaningfulness of an existent in God's Knowledge, as well as all of its inherent events, circumstances, stages, and fruits, visibly demonstrate a sort of life. Being a light emitted by the "Sun" of Eternal Life, life cannot be limited to this world, the present, or to external existence. Rather, each world receives that light's manifestation according to its capacity, and is alive and illumined through it. If this were not so, each world would be a vast and terrible corpse, a dark ruin beneath the visible crust of transient life. This is what the misguided think.

Thus one broad aspect of belief in Divine Destiny and Decree is understood through and established by life's meaning. Just as the life and vitality of the material world and existent, visible objects becomes apparent from their orderliness and the consequences of their existence, past and future creatures (regarded as belonging to the Unseen) have an immaterial existence, an original and spir-

knowledge of them. Past and future, being the two branches of time, is the "realm" where the World of the Absolutely Unseen manifests itself in the visible world, and may be regarded as its second form. (Tr.)

itual presence in God's Knowledge. This is a sort of life. That life and presence attains visible form and is made known via the Tablet of Destiny and Decree, which contains all stages through which beings pass and all events happening to them during their material lives.

Part three

QUESTION: Such verses as: *It is but a single cry* (36:29, 49, 53; 38:15; 54:31) and: *The command of the Hour is but a twinkling of the eye, or nearer* (16:77) show that the Supreme Resurrection will happen in an instant. Our constrained understanding needs a tangible analogy to enable us to concur with and accept such a unique, miraculous event.

ANSWER: The Resurrection comprises three elements [or stages, if time is included]: Spirits will return to their bodies, bodies will be reanimated, and bodies will be rebuilt and resurrected.

FIRST ELEMENT: Imagine the soldiers of a highly disciplined army. Having dispersed in all directions to their separate rest, they can be summoned together with a loud bugle blast. Israfil's trumpet is certainly no less powerful than a bugle.[36] Our spirits—each of which was asked: "Am I not your Lord?" coming from pre-eternity, and affirmed: "Yes, You are" while still in the World of Past Eternity and the Realm of the Particle—are more obedient, disciplined, and submissive than any soldiers.[37]

SECOND ELEMENT: For a celebration in a great city, uncountable lamps may be turned on instantly by flicking a switch in the city's power station. It also would be possible to light an infinite number of lamps throughout the world from a single power station [if one existed]. If electricity, a creation of the All-Mighty, a servant and a candleholder in this temporary world, can manifest this property due to its Creator's training and discipline, the Resurrection can occur in the twinkling of an eye and within the framework of Divine Wisdom's orderly laws, which are represented and demonstrated by thousands of His light-giving servants like electricity.

---

[36] Israfil is the archangel who will blow the Sur (Trumpet) just before the destruction of the universe and the Resurrection, to which the Qur'an alludes in 39:68. (Tr.)

[37] The Thirtieth Word demonstrates that all spirits and particles are obedient troops of a Divine Army.

THIRD ELEMENT: There are thousands of suitable analogies for rebuilding and resurrecting human bodies on the Day of Resurrection. Among them are the way in which tree leaves are restored perfectly (almost identically) to those of the preceding year within a few days after the beginning of each spring, even though trees are far more numerous than people; the way in which all trees' blossoms and fruits are re-created just like those of the preceding spring;[38] the sudden awakening, unfolding, and coming to life of countless seeds, kernels, and roots, all of which are the origin of spring growth; the way in which trees, resembling upright skeletons, abruptly begin to show signs of "resurrection after death"; the reanimation, in a most wonderful way, of countless small creatures, especially of different fly species—their "resurrection" during a few days each spring, together with other insect species, which are far more numerous than all people who have ever lived.

---

[38] Although a tree's leaves, flowers, and fruits are not completely identical to those of the preceding spring, they are not different from them in nature. If they were living and had spirits like human beings, they would be resurrected with the same identity. (Tr.)

This world is the Realm of Wisdom; the Hereafter is the Abode of Power.[39] Here, in accordance with the requirements of such Divine Names as the All-Wise, Arranger, Disposer, Nurturer, and Trainer, creation is extensive and to some degree graduated over time. This is required by His Wisdom as Lord and Sustainer. But given that Power and Mercy are more evident than Wisdom in the Hereafter, creation in that realm is instantaneous and immune to anything related to matter, space, time, and duration.

The Qur'an decrees that what takes a day or a year to create here will be done within an instant there: *The command of the Hour is but a twinkling of the eye, or nearer* (16:77). If you seek a clearer understanding that the Resurrection will come, just as the next spring will, study the Tenth and the Twenty-ninth Words.

Another element of the Resurrection is this world's destruction. If a planet or asteroid collides

---

[39] This world is the Realm of Wisdom, where things happen according to certain purposes and deliberation, in conformity with certain laws, and in which God acts from behind the veil of cause and effect. The Hereafter is the Abode of Power, in which God will act without any veils. (Tr.)

with this planet, by the command of God, our dwelling place will be destroyed instantly, just as a palace that took 10 years to build can be destroyed in a minute.

Part four

> He said: "Who shall revive the bones when they are rotted away?" Say: "The One who originated them the first time shall revive them." He is the Knower of all creation. (36:78-79)

Recall the analogy used in the third comparison in the Ninth Truth of The Tenth Word. In sum: Someone assembles a huge army within one day before your eyes. If you were told that the one who dispersed his troops to different areas for rest could reassemble them and reorder them in battalions, and you replied that he could not, you would be regarded as crazy.

The All-Powerful and All-Knowing, by His command *Be! and it is*, created all animate beings' atoms and subtle bodily constituents out of nothing. He then recorded and assigned them to their places, as if they were an army, with perfect orderliness and balance. During every spring, He creates countless different species and groups of animate crea-

tures, each of which resembles an army. Surely
He can regather, with a blast on Israfil's trumpet,
all the fundamental atoms and original components
that enjoy mutual acquaintance through their collective submission to the body's order—an order
that exceeds that of any battalion. If you consider this improbable, are you not irrational?

In some verses, the All-Mighty tells us what
wonders He has performed here to impress upon
our hearts the wonder of what He will accomplish
in the Hereafter, and to prepare our minds to accept
and understand it. In other verses, He alludes to the
wonderful deeds He will perform in the future and
the Hereafter by analogies with what we see here.
One example is: *Has not humanity seen that We
have created it from a sperm-drop? Then lo, humanity is a manifest adversary* (36:77), and the subsequent verses.

The Wise Qur'an establishes the Resurrection
in seven or eight different forms. It first directs
our attention to our own origin: "You see how you
progressed—from a sperm drop to a blood drop, to
a blood clot suspended on the womb's wall, from
a suspended blood clot to a formless lump of flesh,
and from a formless lump of flesh to a human

form.[40] How can you deny your second creation? It is just the same as the first, or even easier [for God to accomplish]."

God also refers to the great bounties He has granted to us: *He Who made fire for you from the green tree* (36:80). He asks us: "Will the One Who has bestowed His bounty upon you leave you free to behave as you wish and then enter the grave to sleep permanently without rising again?" The Qur'an teaches us by the following similitude: You see trees come to life again and grow green. Your bones resemble dry branches, yet you refuse to recognize the likeness in their reanimation and regard such a thing as utterly improbable.

The Qur'an asks: "Could the One Who creates the heavens and Earth not have power over humanity's life and death, since we are the fruit of the heavens and Earth? Do you seriously suppose that He would render futile and fruitless the Tree of

---

[40] *We created humanity from an extraction of clay, then We set him, a sperm-drop, in a safe lodging, then We created of the drop a blood clot suspended on the wall of the womb, then We created of the suspended blood clot a little lump, then We created of the little lump bones, then We clothed the bones in flesh; thereafter We produced him as another creature* (23:12-14). (Tr.)

Creation, all of whose parts He shaped with purposive wisdom, by forsaking its high purpose and issue: humanity?" It replies: "The One Who will restore you to life at the Resurrection is the One before Whom all creation is like His obedient soldier. It bows its head submissively whenever it hears the command *'Be!' and it is."* Creating spring is as easy for Him as creating a flower, and creating all animals is as easy for His Power as creating a fly. No one should defy or diminish His Power by demanding: "Who will revive the bones?"

In: *Glory be to Him in Whose hand is the dominion over all things* (36:83), the Qur'an affirms His control and possession of the key to all things. He replaces night with day, winter with summer, as easily as turning a page in a book. He is All-Powerful, Majestic. He closes up the world and opens the Hereafter as if they were no more than two stations. Given this: *To Him you shall be returned* (36:83). Thus He will revive you, take you to the Plain of Resurrection, and judge you in His majestic Presence.

Such analogies prepare our hearts and minds to accept the Resurrection. However, the Qur'an sometimes alludes to God's actions in the Hereafter in a way calling attention to their worldly par-

allels, so that no room is left for doubt and denial.
Examples are found in the *sura*s opened by: *When
the sun is folded up* (81:1), *When the heavens are
torn asunder* (82:1), and *When the heavens are
torn apart* (84:1). In these *sura*s, the All-Mighty
alludes to the Resurrection and the vast revolutions,
as well as the Lordly deeds that will occur then, by
analogies with what we see every autumn or spring.
Understanding these analogies, which inspire awe
in our hearts, we can accept easily that which the
intellect might otherwise refuse. As a more detailed
analysis would occupy many pages, we will con-
fine ourselves to: *When the pages are spread out*
(81:10).

This verse implies: "At the time of the Resurrection, everyone's deeds will be revealed on a
written page." At first glance, this appears rather
strange and incomprehensible. But as the *sura* indicates, just as spring's renewal parallels another
resurrection, the "spreading out of the pages" has
a very clear parallel. Every fruit-bearing tree and
flowering plant has its properties, functions, and
deeds. It performs its worship according to the kind
of its glorification of God (namely, manifesting
His Names).

All of its deeds and its life's record are inscribed in each seed that will emerge next spring in another plot of soil. With the tongue of shape and form, the trees or flowering plants [growing from seeds buried the previous autumn] eloquently point to the original tree's or flowering plant's life and deeds, and spread out the pages of their deeds through their branches, twigs, leaves, blossoms, and fruits. He Who says: *When the pages are spread out* is the same Being Who, before our eyes, achieves these feats in a very wise, prudent, efficient, and subtle way. Such a way is dictated by His Names the All-Wise, All-Preserving, All-Sustaining and Training, and All-Subtle.[41]

You can pursue other issues of the Resurrection through similar analogies. For example, consider that: *When the sun is folded up* (81:1) both refers to a brilliant image, through *folded up* also alludes to its parallel in this world:

_____

[41] Since the Qur'an addresses all times and peoples of different level of understanding, it naturally could not be expected to explain how the recording and reproduction of sounds and images will take place. However, humanity's ability to do such things via tape recorders and television is a decisive argument for the "spreading out of the pages" of people's deeds on the Day of Judgment. (Tr.)

FIRST: The All-Mighty drew aside the veils of non-being, then of ether and the heavens, to bring forth from His Mercy's treasury and show the world a jewel-like lamp—the sun—to lighten that world. After closing the world, He will wrap that jewel again in its veils and remove it.

SECOND: The sun may be considered an official tasked with diffusing light and alternately winding light and darkness around Earth's head. Every evening, it is ordered to gather up its commodity (light) and be concealed. Sometimes the sun does only a little business, because a cloud or the moon might form a veil that prevents it from carrying out its task completely. Just as the sun has its goods and ledgers gathered up regularly in this world, a day will come when it will be relieved of its duties.

Even if there were no reason for such a dismissal, the two spots on its face—now small and liable to grow—may grow to the point that the sun will take back, by its Lord's command, the light that it wraps around Earth's head. God will wrap that light around the sun's own head, saying: "Come, you have no more duty toward Earth. Journey to Hell and burn its inhabitants, those who worshipped you and thus insulted an obedient servant like you with faithlessness." With its dark, scarred face, the sun announces the decree: *When the sun is folded up* (81:1).

Part five

All 124,000 Prophets, the elect of humanity, have reported that the Hereafter exists and that all beings will be taken there, just as the Creator has promised. These reports are based on their direct vision and absolute conviction. Millions of saints confirm these reports based on their knowledge and their unveiling and experiencing of (hidden truths), and testify to the existence of the Hereafter.

All Names of the universe's All-Wise Maker require the existence of an eternal realm through their manifestations displayed in this world. In addition, the Hereafter's existence is required for the following reasons:

- The infinite Eternal Power, which each spring revives countless dead trees and different plant and animal species (all "specimens" of the ultimate Resurrection) with *"Be!" and it is*, thereby making them images of the Resurrection, requires it.

- The limitless Everlasting Wisdom's attention to the least detail over an infinite extent requires it.

- The Eternal Mercy and Permanent Favoring that sustain, with perfect caring and in a wonderful fashion, all animate beings in need of provision, and that display each spring an infinite diversity of adornment and beauty within a short period, require it.

- Our ardent, irremovable, and persistent love of eternity, our longing for immortality, our desire for permanence, and the facts that we are the most beloved of God's creatures and are more concerned with creation than any other being require it.

From this we can understand that the existence of an eternal Hereafter, including a Realm of Happiness, is evidently shown and firmly established. This is proven so effectively that we must accept it, just as we accept this world's existence.[42]

---

[42] It may be realized from this part how easy it is to report an already existing thing or clear fact and how hard it is to deny it. For example, if someone says: "Somewhere on this Earth is a wonderful garden that provides "canned" milk—all kinds of fruit—and others dispute this, the first person only has to show the garden or some of its produce. Deniers, however, must inspect and display the whole world to justify

Belief in the Hereafter is one of the most important lessons taught by the Wise Qur'an. It is so firm and contains such a powerful hope and consolation that it will console an elderly person. Saying: "Praise be to God for the perfection of belief," we, the elderly, should rejoice in our old age.

---

their negation. Similarly, the testimony of two truthful witnesses (such as Prophets or saints) establishes Paradise's existence, even if we do not consider the many signs and indications demonstrated by others who assert its existence. Deniers must examine, explore, and sift the infinite cosmos and travel throughout infinite and eternal time before they can prove Paradise's non-existence. Therefore, my friends, understand how secure and sound it is to believe in the Hereafter.

Answers to Questions about Paradise

In the Name of God, the Merciful, the Compassionate.

Give glad tidings to those who believe and do good deeds. For them are Gardens underneath which rivers flow. Every time they are provided with fruit thereof, they say: "This is what we were provided with before," and it is given to them in resemblance. There are pure spouses for them, and they shall abide there forever. (2:25)

Below are brief answers to questions about Paradise, which is everlasting. The Qur'anic descriptions, which are more beautiful than Paradise, more delightful than its houris, and sweeter than its springs' pleasant water, leave nothing to be added. We shall point out some steps so that such brilliant, eternal, elevated, and beautiful verses can be understood easily. We also shall explain some fine points, resembling flowers from that Qur'anic paradise, through five significant questions and answers.

Paradise is the means of all spiritual and bodily pleasures

QUESTION: What does the defective, changing, unstable, and pain-stricken body have to do with eternity and Paradise? The spirit's elevated pleasures must be enough. Why should a bodily resurrection take place for bodily pleasures?

ANSWER: Soil, despite its darkness and density when compared to water, air, and light, is the means and source of all works of Divine art. Therefore it is somehow superior in meaning over other elements. Your selfhood, despite its density and due to its being comprehensive and provided it is purified, gains some kind of superiority over your other senses and faculties. Likewise, your body is a most comprehensive and rich mirror for the Divine Names' manifestations, and has been equipped with instruments to weigh and measure the contents of all Divine treasuries. For example, if the tongue's sense of taste were not the origin of as many measures as the varieties of food and drink, it could not experience, recognize, or measure them. Furthermore, your body also contains the instruments needed to experience and recognize most of the Divine Names' manifestations, as well as the faculties for experiencing the most various and infinitely different pleasures.

The universe's conduct and humanity's comprehensive nature show that the Maker of the universe wants to make known all His Mercy's treasuries and all His Names' manifestations, and to make us experience all His bounties by means of the universe. Given this, as the World of Eternal Happiness is a mighty pool into which the flood of the universe flows, a vast exhibition of what the loom of the universe produces, and the everlasting store of crops produced in the field of this (material) world, it will resemble the universe to some degree. The All-Wise Maker, the All-Compassionate Just One, will give pleasures particular to each bodily organ as wages for their duty, service, and worship. To think otherwise would be contrary to His Wisdom, Justice, and Compassion.

QUESTION: A living body is in a state of formation and deformation, and so is subject to disintegration and is non-eternal. Eating and drinking perpetuate the individual; sexual relations perpetuate the species. These are fundamental to life in this world, but are irrelevant and unnecessary in the World of Eternity. Given this, why have they been included among Paradise's greatest pleasures?

ANSWER: A living body declines and dies because the balance between what it needs to maintain and takes in is disturbed. From childhood until the age of physical maturity, it takes in more than it lets out and grows healthier. Afterwards, it usually cannot meet its needs in a balanced way. Either it takes in more than what it needs and so become fat, or takes in less than it needs and so becomes thin. This causes the balance to be destroyed and, in normal circumstances, finally leads to death. In the World of Eternity, however, the body's particles remain constant and are immune to disintegration and re-formation. In other words, this balance remains constant.[43]

---

[43] In this world, human and animal bodies are like guesthouses, barracks, or schools for atoms. Lifeless atoms enter them, become worthy of being atoms for the eternal world, and then leave them. In the Hereafter, however, according to: *The Abode of the Hereafter—it is all living indeed* (29:64), the light of life encompasses everything. There is no need for its atoms to make the same journey and undergo the same training as atoms in this world must do.

Like moving in perpetual cycles, a living body gains eternity together with the constant operation of the factory of bodily life for pleasure. In this world, eating, drinking, and marital sexual relations arise from a need and perform a function. Thus a great variety of excellent (and superior) pleasures are ingrained in them as immediate wages for the functions performed. In this world of ailments, eating and marriage lead to many wonderful and various pleasures. Thus Paradise, the Realm of Happiness and Pleasure, must contain these pleasures in their most elevated form. Adding to them otherworldly wages (as pleasures) for the duties performed in the world by them and the need felt for them here in the form of a pleasant and otherworldly appetite, they will be transformed into an all-encompassing, living source of pleasure that is appropriate to Paradise and eternity.

According to: *The life of this world is but a pastime and a game, but the Abode of the Hereafter— it is all living indeed* (29:64), all lifeless and unconscious substances and objects in this world are living and conscious in the other world. Like people and animals here, trees and stones there will understand and obey commands. If you tell a tree to bring you such-and-such a fruit, it will do so. If you tell a stone to come, it will come. Since stones and trees will assume such an elevated form, it will be necessary for eating, drinking, and marital relations to assume a form that is superior to their worldly forms to the same degree as Paradise is superior to this world. This includes preserving their bodily realities.

QUESTION: A Tradition states that "a person is with the one he or she loves," and so friends will be together in Paradise. Thus a simple Bedouin who feels a deep love for God's Messenger in one minute of companionship with him should be together with him in Paradise. But how can a simple nomad's illumination and reward cause him to share the same place with God's Messenger, whose illumination and reward are limitless?

ANSWER: I shall point to this elevated truth by a comparison. A magnificent person prepared a vast banquet and a richly adorned event in an extremely beautiful and splendid garden. It included all delicious foods that taste can experience, all beautiful things that please sight, all wonders that amuse the imagination, and so on. Everything that would gratify and please the external and inner senses was present. Two friends went to the banquet and sat at a table in the same pavilion. One had only limited taste and so received little pleasure. His weak sight and inability to smell prevented him from understanding the wonderful arts or comprehending the marvels. He could benefit only to the degree of his capacity, which was miniscule. But the other person had developed his external and internal senses, intellect, heart, and all faculties and feelings to the utmost degree. Therefore he could perceive, experience, and derive pleasure from all subtleties, beauties, marvels, and fine things in that exquisite garden.

This is how it is in our confused, painful, and narrow world. There is an infinite distance between the greatest and the least, who exist side by side in Paradise, the Abode of Happiness and Eternity. While friends are together, it is more fitting that each receives his or her share from the table of the Most Merciful of the Merciful according to the degree of his or her ability. Even though they are in different Paradises or on different "floors" of Paradise, they will be able to meet, for Paradise's eight levels are one above the other and share the same roof—the Supreme Throne of God.

Suppose there are walled circles around a conical mountain, one within the other and one above the other, each one facing another, from its foot to the summit. This does not prevent each one from seeing the sun. (Indeed, various narrations or Traditions indicate that the levels or floors of Paradise are somewhat like this.)

QUESTION: Prophetic Traditions say: "Houris are clothed in 70 garments (one over the other), yet the marrow of their leg-bones may be seen." What does this mean? What sort of beauty is this?

ANSWER: This Tradition has a fine meaning and a lovely beauty. In this world, which is ugly, lifeless, and for the most part just a covering, it is sufficient as long as beauty and loveliness appear to the eye as beautiful and until too much familiarity conceals it. In Paradise, which is beautiful, living, brilliant, and entirely essence or kernel without covering, like the eye, all our senses and faculties will want to receive their different pleasures from houris and from the women coming from this world, who will be even more beautiful than houris. This Tradition *indicates* that from the beauty of the top garment to the marrow in the bone, each will be the means of pleasure for a sense and faculty.

It also points out that the houris' adornment, physical and spiritual beauty and charm, will please, satisfy, and gratify all the yearnings of our senses, feelings, powers, and faculties for beauty, and their great fondness for pleasure and adornment. Clothed in 70 sorts of adornment of Paradise in such a way that one does not conceal another, houris display more than 70 sorts of bodily and spiritual beauty and elegance, and thereby demonstrate the truth contained in: *In it (Paradise) is whatever the souls desire and the eyes delight in* (43:71).[44]

This Tradition also points out that since Paradise contains no unnecessary, peeled, or shelled waste

---

[44] The greatest blessing in Paradise is obtaining God's approval and good pleasure and, as implied by some verses and explicitly stated in some Traditions, seeing God beyond all concepts of quality and quantity. However, since such purely spiritual blessings are concerned rather with the élite of the believers, the Qur'an usually mentions the blessings of Paradise as if they were purely bodily pleasures. People are not composed of only the spirit, but are tripartite beings composed of a spirit, carnal soul, and flesh (the physical body). Since believers' bodies and carnal souls serve them in the world, have to endure some hardships, and are deprived of some of the worldly pleasures to be disciplined and trained, each body will be rewarded with the pleasures particular to them. However, it must not be thought that those pleasures are purely corporeal.

matter with sediment, its inhabitants will not excrete
waste after eating and drinking. In this world, trees,
the most ordinary of living beings, do not excrete
despite taking in much nourishment. So why should
Paradise's inhabitants, the highest category of life,
excrete waste?

QUESTION: Some Prophetic Traditions say that
some inhabitants of Paradise will be given a place

The spiritual contentment they will give is greater than the
corporeal satisfaction. For example, every person needs a
friend, a companion. What most satisfies a person's human
needs is having an intimate life companion with whom to
share love, joy, and grief. Since the kindest and most compassionate and generous of hearts is the heart of a woman,
the Qur'an mentions women as among the greatest blessings of Paradise for men, rather than vice versa. That is, in
addition to the sensual pleasure she provides, the spiritual
pleasure she can give to her spouse through such elevated
feelings as compassion, love, and being a life-companion is
greater than a man can give her. This does not mean that women
in Paradise will be left without companions. The pleasure
coming from mutual helping, sharing the joy and grief of one
another and companionship, and that provided by love, affection, and intimacy, is much greater that the bodily pleasures
men and women supply for each other. Those defeated by
bodily pleasures and unaware of the spiritual pleasures included in them may see Paradise—mistakenly—as a realm of sensual enjoyment. (Tr.)

as large as the world, and that hundreds of thousands of palaces and houris will be granted to them. What is the reason for this, and why and how does one person need all these things?

ANSWER: If you were only a solid object, a vegetable creature consisting of a stomach, or only had a limited, heavy, simple, and transient corporal or animal body, you would not own or deserve so many palaces or houris. But you are a comprehensive miracle of Divine Power. If you ruled this world and used all of its wealth and pleasure to satisfy your undeveloped senses' and faculties' needs, you still could not satisfy your greed during your brief life. However, if you have an infinite capacity in an eternal abode of happiness, and if you knock on the door of infinite Mercy in the tongue of infinite need, you will receive the Divine bounties described in such Traditions. We shall present a comparison to illustrate this elevated truth.

Like this valley garden, each vineyard and garden in Barla has a different owner.[45] Each bird, sparrow, or honey-bee, which has only a handful of

---

[45] This garden in Barla belongs to Süleyman, who served this poor one with perfect loyalty for 8 years, where this Word was written in 1 or 2 hours.

grain, may say: "All of Barla's vineyards and gardens are my places of recreation." Each may possess Barla and include it in its property. The fact that others share it does not negate its rule. A truly human person may say: "My Creator made the world a home for me, with the sun as its chief lamp and the stars as its electric lights. Earth is my cradle spread with flowered carpets," and then thanks God. This conclusion is not negated because other creatures live in this "house." On the contrary, the creatures adorn this home and are like its decorations. If, on account of being human, you or even a bird were to claim the right of control over such a vast area in this narrow, brief world and to receive such a vast bounty, why should you consider it unlikely that you will own property stretching for 500 years in a broad, eternal abode of happiness?[46]

Just as the sun is present here in many mirrors simultaneously, a spiritually enlightened being may be present in many places at the same time, as discussed in The Sixteenth Word. For example, Gabriel can be on 1,000 stars while being present at God's Supreme Throne, in the Prophet's pres-

---

[46] In classical jurisprudential books, a day's distance is about 30 kms (about 18.6 miles). (Tr.)

ence, and in the Divine Presence. Prophet Muhammad can meet with most of the devoted, God-conscious members of his community in the Place of Gathering after the Resurrection, just as he can appear in many places and to numerous saintly people in this world simultaneously. A group of saints (*abdal*: substitutes) can appear in many places at the same moment. Ordinary people sometimes can do as much as a year's work in a minute while dreaming or having a vision of it, and everyone can be in contact with and concerned with many places at the same time in heart, in spirit, and in imagination. Such things are well-known and witnessed.

Given this, the inhabitants of Paradise (which is of light, unrestricted, broad, and eternal) will have bodies with the spirit's strength and lightness and the imagination's swiftness. They will be able to be in countless places simultaneously, talk with innumerable houris, and receive pleasure in an infinite number of ways. This is fitting for that eternal Paradise and infinite Mercy, and the Truthful Reporter says that this is the reality and the truth. But such truths cannot be weighed on the scales of our tiny minds.

Glory be to You. We have no knowledge save only what You have taught us. You are the All-Knowing, All-Wise.

O Lord, do not call us to account if we forget or fall into error. O God, bestow blessings on Your beloved, who opened the doors of Paradise through being beloved by You, and through his prayers, and whose community You enabled to open those doors through calling Your blessings on him. On him be blessings and peace. O God, let us enter Paradise among the pure, righteous ones through the intercession of Your chosen beloved. Amin.

Doomsday, the World's Destruction, and the Afterlife

This chapter consists of an introduction and four fundamentals.

Introduction: If one were to claim that a city or a palace will be destroyed and then reconstructed firmly, one would be asked the following six questions:

- Why will it be destroyed, and is its destruction necessary?
- Can its destroyer and its rebuilder really do these things?
- Is such destruction possible?
- If possible, will it really be destroyed?
- Is such rebuilding possible?
- If possible, will it actually be rebuilt?

The world is equivalent to a palace, and the universe to a city. Both can be destroyed, and there is a necessary cause for their destruction. Their destroyer and rebuilder can do both.

FIRST FUNDAMENTAL: The spirit is eternal, and the First Aim's proofs for the existence of angels and other spirit beings prove its eternity. We are too close to the souls of the dead, who are waiting in the *barzakh*[47] to go to the Hereafter, to require proof of their existence. If such beings have the necessary insight into the reality of things, saints may see and even communicate with them. In addition, almost everyone encounters them in true dreams. As modern materialism causes doubt in such obvious matters, we provide four sources from which persuasive knowledge can be obtained.

Introduction: An eternal, matchless beauty requires an eternal lover through whom it will be reflected permanently. A faultless, eternal, and perfect art demands a permanent contemplative herald. An infinite mercy and benevolence require the continued ease and happiness of needy ones to thank it. The human soul is the foremost of those lovers, contemplative heralds, and needy thank-

---

[47] The intermediate world between this world and the next. (Ed.)

ful ones. Given this, it will accompany that beauty, perfection, and mercy on the way to eternity.

Perhaps all creatures, even the most primitive, are created for some kind of eternity. Even the spiritless flower has a sort of post-death immortality: Its form is preserved in memories, and the laws of its formation gain permanence via new flowers growing from its seeds. Since these laws, the model of its form that has the same significance for it as our spirit has for us, is preserved through its seeds by the All-Preserving, All-Wise One, the human soul, which has a sublime comprehensive nature and consciousness and has been clothed with external existence, is far more deserving of being eternal. How could an All-Wise One of Majesty, an All-Preserving One of Eternity, Who maintains a huge tree's life-cycle and the law of its formation through a tiny seed, not preserve the souls of dead people?

First source: This concerns you as an individual and relates to your inner world. Look carefully into your life and inner aspect, and you will discern the existence of an eternal spirit. Every person changes his or her body annually through a complete renewal, but the spirit remains unchanged.

The body is ephemeral; the spirit inhabiting it is permanent. The formation or deformation of your body's molecules, or its composition and decomposition, does not affect the spirit, which annually changes or renews its bodily garment. When it strips off this garment at the time of death, neither its permanence nor its essential nature are affected because, as established through experiences and observation, the spirit does not depend upon the body for its life. The body is only its dwelling place, not its cover. The spirit has a subtle cover, its "energetic envelope," and leaves its dwelling place dressed in this cover when its body dies.

Second source: This relates to the outer world. Observation and experience indicate the spirit's eternity. The individual spirit's permanence, which has been established in the afterlife, confirms the soul's perpetuation after death. It has been established logically that any essential aspect observed in an individual is common to the whole species, for qualities originating in the essence are shared by all individuals. Each soul's permanent existence after the body's death, as based on observation and countless experiences in dreams and other kinds of communication, is as certain as the existence of a continent that we have never visited. They have a relationship with us, for our prayers reach them and we receive their blessing in return. Moreover, it can be perceived that an essential aspect of each person exists after physical death: his or her spirit.

As the spirit is a simple unitary entity, it is not subject to disintegration or decomposition like composite material things. Life ensures a form of unity within multiplicity and causes a sort of permanence. In other words, unity and permanence are essential to the spirit, from which they spread to multiplicity.

The spirit's mortality would be due either to its decomposition and disintegration or its annihilation. The first option is impossible, for the spirit has a simple unitary essence. The second option also is impossible, for it is contrary to the Absolutely All-Generous One's infinite Mercy. Moreover, His boundless Munificence would not allow the human spirit to be deprived of the blessing of existence that He has bestowed on it, for it ardently desires and is worthy of this blessing.

Third source: The spirit is a living, conscious, light-giving entity; a comprehensive law or command of God furnished with external existence and has the potential to achieve universality. Even natural laws, which are considerably weak when compared to the spirit, have stability and permanence, let alone the law embodied by the spirit. All kinds of existence, although subject to change, possess a permanent dimension that remains unaltered through all stages of life. Thus each person is an individual and, on account of his or her comprehensive nature, universal consciousness, and all-embracing imagination, like a species. A law that operates upon humanity also applies to the individual.

The Majestic Creator endowed us with a sublime nature and caused us to be comprehensive mirrors through which His Names and Attributes are reflected. He has charged us with a universal duty of worship. Given this, each individual's spiritual reality remains alive forever by Divine permission, even though its form undergoes countless changes. Thus the human spirit, which constitutes our conscious, living element, is eternal and has been made so by God's command and permission.

Fourth source: The Divine laws of nature resemble the spirit, for they also belong to the world of the Divine Will and Command. However, they operate upon categories that do not have a perceptive existence. When we analyze these laws, we see that they would have been the spirits of the categories themselves if they had been given external existence. As they are permanent and unchanging, their unity is not affected by any alteration or transformation. The seeds of a dead fig tree still contain the permanent, spirit-like law relating to its formation.

Since weak and ordinary commanding laws are connected to permanence and continuance, the human spirit must be connected to permanence and immortality—and eternity. According to: *The spirit is of My Lord's Command* (17:85), the spirit is a conscious and living law from the world of Divine Command and has been endowed with external existence by Eternal Power. Since unconscious laws issuing from the Divine Attribute of Will and the World of Divine Command are permanent, the spirit is even worthier of such permanence, for it comes from the same source and has the additional attributes of life and possessing an external reality. Being conscious means that it is more sublime and powerful than other laws; having life means that it is more permanent and valuable than them.

SECOND FUNDAMENTAL: An eternal World of Happiness is necessary, and the Majestic One can create it. Both the destruction of our universe as well as the resurrection of everything are possible and will occur. The following remarks remove all doubt concerning the Resurrection, and the following 10 points explain the purpose and necessary cause for an eternal World of Happiness:

First point: Creation displays a perfect harmony and a purposeful order, and every aspect of the universe shows signs of a will and indications of a purpose. It is impossible not to discern a wisdom and choice in each thing and event, intention and will, and in each composition through the testimony of its fruits or results. If creation were not meant to produce eternal happiness, its harmony and order would be a deceit. In addition, all meanings, relations, and connections (the spirit of order) would come to nothing, for only eternal happiness causes this order to be established.

Second point: The universe's creation displays perfect wisdom. Divine Wisdom, the representation of eternal favor, proclaims the coming of eternal happiness through the tongue of observing benefits and purposes throughout the universe. If there were no eternal happiness, all benefits and purposes observed in the universe would have to be denied.

Third point: Human intellect, wisdom, experience, and deductive reasoning point out that nothing superfluous or vain occurs in creation. This indicates the existence of eternal happiness. The universe's Majestic Maker chooses the best and easiest way in creation, and apportions many duties and purposes to each creature, no matter how insignificant it may appear. Since there is no waste and nothing in vain, there must be eternal happiness, for eternal non-existence would make everything futile and wasteful. The absence of waste in creation, particularly in humanity, demonstrates that our countless spiritual potentialities, limitless aspirations and ideas, and inclinations will never go to waste. Our basic inclination toward perfection indicates perfection's existence, and our desire for happiness proclaims that we are destined for eternal happiness. If this were not so, all basic spiritual features and sublime aspirations constituting our true nature would be wasteful and futile.

Fourth point: The alternation of day and night, as well as spring and winter, atmospheric changes, our body's annual renewal, and our awakening and rising every morning after sleep all indicate a complete rising and renewal. Seconds forecast a minute, a minute predicts an hour, and an hour anticipates a day. The dials of God's great clock—Earth—point, in succession, to the day, the year, our lifetime, and the ages through which the world passes. As they show morning after night and spring after winter, they intimate that the morning of the Resurrection will follow the death of creation.

A person's life contains many cycles that can be regarded as a kind of death and resurrection (e.g., daily, seasonal, and annual changes; sleeping and waking; and various revivals and renewals). Nature's revival every spring is a promise of the final Resurrection, for during that season countless kinds of resurrection take place among animals and plants. Thus the All-Wise Creator reminds us of the Resurrection to come.

All people are equal in value and comprehensiveness to any other animate species, because the light of their intellect has endowed them with comprehensive aspirations and ideas encompassing the past and the future. In all other species, an individual's nature is particular, its value is personal, its view is restricted, its qualities are limited, and its pleasure and pain are instantaneous. Human beings, however, have a sublime nature and the greatest value, limitless perfection, and a more permanent spiritual pleasure and pain. Given this, the kinds of resurrection experienced by other species suggest that every human being will be resurrected completely on the Day of Judgment.

Fifth point: Humanity is endowed with unlimited potentialities that develop into unrestricted abilities. These, in turn, give rise to countless inclinations that generate limitless desires, which are the source of infinite ideas and concepts. All of these, as observed and confirmed by scholars of profound knowledge, indicate the existence of a World of Eternal Happiness beyond this material world. Our innate inclination toward eternal happiness makes one sure that such a world will be established.

Sixth point: The all-encompassing mercy of the universe's All-Merciful Maker requires a World of Eternal Happiness. Were it not for this happiness, God's chief grace for humanity, all people would raise lamentations over eternal separation, acts of favor would turn into vengeance, and Divine Compassion would be negated. But Divine Mercy is found throughout creation and is more evident than the sun. Observe the three manifestations of Divine Compassion: love, affection, and intellect. If human life resulted in eternal separation with unending pangs of parting, that gracious love would turn into the greatest affliction, affection into a most painful ailment, and the light-giving intellect into an unmitigated evil. Divine Compassion, however, (for it is Compassion) never inflicts the agony of eternal separation upon true love.

Seventh point: All known pleasure-giving experiences, beauties, perfections, attractions, ardent yearnings, and feelings of compassion are spiritual articulations and manifestations of the Majestic Creator's Favor, Mercy, and Munificence made known to the intellect. Since there is a truth and a reality in this universe, there is true Mercy; since there is true Mercy, there will be eternal happiness.

Eighth point: Our conscience (conscious nature) indicates eternal happiness. Whoever listens to it hears it saying eternity over and over again. Even if we were given the entire universe, we would not be compensated for the lack of eternity, for we have an innate longing and were created for it. Thus our natural inclination toward eternal happiness comes from an objective reality—eternity's existence and our desire for eternity.

Ninth point: The Prophet, who spoke the truth and whose words have been confirmed throughout the centuries, preached and promised the coming of everlasting life and eternal happiness. His message concentrated almost as much on the Resurrection as on Divine Unity, referring to the consensus of all Prophets and saints.

Tenth point: The Qur'an, a matchless miracle with 40 aspects, announces the Resurrection and the coming of eternal happiness. It unveils creation's mystery and offers uncountable rational arguments for the Resurrection. Such verses as: *He created you by stages* (71:14) and *Say: "He Who has originated them the first time shall bring them to life again"* (36:79) contain a comparison and an analogy. And, *Your Lord does not wrong His servants* (41:46) indicates God's justice. These provide us with a view of the Resurrection and everlasting happiness. I have discussed the proofs within these verses in my treatise *Nukta* (The Point) as follows:

Each human being undergoes ordered and systematic changes during the process of development. Each sperm, blood-clot, tissue, bone, and flesh that develops (in stages) into another (distinct) human-shaped being must adhere to precise principles that, particular to the successive stages of development, indicate the exercise of purpose, will, and wisdom. The All-Wise Creator, Who creates human beings by these stages, also causes the body to renew itself each year. This renewal demands the replacement of decomposed cells by new ones produced by the All-Provident One's provision of food according to the needs of each bodily part.

If we observe the atoms used to renew or repair the body, we see them come together from the atmosphere, soil, and water. Their motions are so precise that it seems they have received marching orders to go to a certain place. In addition, their manner of going indicates the operation of the Real Agent. Starting from the inanimate world of elements and chemical substances, they pass into the animated world of vegetables and animals. Having developed into *sustenance* in agreement with definite principles, they enter the body as food. After being "cooked" in different "kitchens" and transformed and passed through some "filters," they are distributed to the body's parts according to need.[48]

All of these processes take place in accordance with the All-Provident One's laws and without the intervention of blind chance, lawless coincidence, deaf nature, and unconscious causes. They display perfect knowledge, wisdom, and insight. At whatever stage an atom enters the body's cell from the surrounding element, it does so in an orderly fashion and conforms to that stage's specified laws. To whichever level it travels, it steps with such order that it appears self-evidently to be proceeding at an All-Wise Mover's command. Never deviating from its aim and object, it gradually advances from stage to stage and from level to level until, at the command of its Sustainer, it reaches its appropriate position. Once there, it establishes itself and begins to work.

The provision of food and its reaching the cells for which it is destined show Divine Will and Divine Determination. So perfect is this process'

---

[48] A reference to the organs and systems involved in digesting, breathing, and filtering what is consumed. (Tr.)

order and arrangement that each particle seems to have its final destination written on its "forehead." Is it conceivable that the Majestic Creator, Who exercises Lordship over creation with boundless power and all-encompassing wisdom, from particles of matter to planets, and spins them with order and balance, could fail to revive creation? Qur'anic verses open our eyes to this revival by comparing it with our first creation:

> Say: "He Who has originated them the first time (with definite purpose) will bring them to life again (in the Hereafter)." (36:79)

> He originates creation, then brings it back again, and it is easier for Him. (30:27)

Soldiers of a battalion come together again at a bugle call more rapidly than when they had dispersed to rest. Such a feat is as easy and possible for a body's essential particles, which had established mutual close relations and familiarity during their worldly life, when the angel Israfil blows his trumpet. In fact, they can do so more readily than at the first creation. Not all of the component parts even have to be present; rather, the fundamental parts and essential particles, which are like nuclei and seeds and which a Prophetic Tradition calls "the root of the tail" (the *os coccyx*), may suffice for the second creation's basis and foundation. The All-Wise Creator will rebuild the human body upon this foundation.

The following section summarizes the truth expressed by the analogy of justice in such verses as: *Your Lord does not wrong His servants* (41:46).

We observe that cruel, sinful, and tyrannical persons usually lead a comfortable and luxurious life while godly, oppressed people live in poverty and difficulty. Death makes them equal, for both would have departed forever with their deeds unquestioned if there were no supreme tribunal. Divine Wisdom and Justice, which allow no wrong-doing to go unnoticed and forbid injustice, require the establishment of a supreme tribunal to punish evil and reward good.

As this world is not exactly propitious for a complete development of human potentialities, we are destined to find realization in another world. Our essence is comprehensive and is bound for eternity. As our nature is basically sublime, we can accomplish important things, whether good or evil. Order and discipline are essential, and we should not be left to ourselves to deteriorate into non-existence. Hell is waiting for us with a wide-open mouth, and Paradise is expecting us with open arms.

Study the verses like the two mentioned above, which contain rational arguments for the Resurrection, and see what a great truth is contained in eternal life. The Ten Points you have been following also give you a clear insight and strong evidence for the Resurrection. Moreover, the Majestic Creator's Beautiful Names (e.g., All-Wise, All-Compassionate, All-Preserver, and All-Just) actually require that the Resurrection should occur, that eternal life should come, and that eternal happiness should be realized. Consequently, the Resurrection's necessity and requirement is so strong that there is no room for doubt or uncertainty.

THIRD FUNDAMENTAL: Just as the Resurrection's necessity and requirement is certain, so the One Who will bring it about can do so. As He has power over everything, everything is the same in relation to His Power. He creates the spring as easily as a flower. He is so powerful that creation bears witness to His Power and Majesty. Given this, how can you doubt that He can raise the dead for the Last Judgment? His Power is so great that He causes a new environment to come into existence each century, renews the universe every year, and creates a new world every day. He hangs many transient worlds upon the string of time as centuries, years, or even days pass for a perfect, definite purpose. He displays His Wisdom's perfection and His art's beauty by clothing Earth in the garment of spring as if it were a single flower, and then decorating and embellishing it with countless examples of resurrection.

Since He can do such things, how can you doubt His ability to bring about the Resurrection and replace this world with another? The verse: *Your creation and your being raised up are as but the creation and raising up of a single soul* (31:28) announces that the All-Powerful One is so powerful that nothing is difficult for Him, that creating innumerable individuals is as easy creating one.

Divine Power comes from the Divine Essence's very nature, and so there can be no incapacity connected with It. As it operates the inner, immaterial dimension of existence, no obstacle can interfere with Its operation. In Its relation to things, Divine Power resembles the Divine laws of nature, which say that creating a universal thing is as easy as creating a particular thing. Consider the following arguments:

First argument: Eternal Power is essential to Divine Essence, for it is an indispensable attribute of Divinity. They are identical in one respect: Any incapacity is impossible, for this would presuppose the existence of two opposites in the Infinite Being. Since this is impossible, and since impotence cannot occur in the Divine Essence, nothing can interfere with Divine Power. Since impotence cannot be involved with Divine Power, it can have no degrees, for such degrees of a thing's existence come about only through the intervention of opposites. Degrees of temperature occur because of cold's intervention, and degrees of beauty exist because of ugliness' intervention. This is true of all qualities in the universe. Contingent things and beings contain opposites, for they do not exist essentially of themselves and no undiluted quality is essential to their existence. As the World of Contingencies contains degrees and graduations, it is subject to change and transformation.

Since Eternal Divine Power contains no degrees, it is equally easy for it to create or bring into existence particles or galaxies. Resurrecting humanity is as easy for it as reviving one person, and creating spring is as easy as creating a flower. If creation or resurrection were ascribed to causes, creating a flower would be as difficult as creating spring. But if there is only One Creator, creating everything is as easy as creating one thing.

Second argument: Divine Power operates in the inner, spiritual dimension of things (the metaphysical kingdom). Like a mirror, the universe has two sides: corporeal (resembling a mirror's colored face) and metaphysical (resembling the mirror's shining face and looking to the Creator). Opposites exist in the corporeal side, which manifests beauty and ugliness, good and bad, big and small, difficulty and ease. The Majestic Creator of the universe veils His Power's acts behind the veil of observed causes so that those who lack understanding do not regard His Power's relation to simple things as unbecoming to Him. His Honor and Majesty require this. Causes have no real effect upon creation, for that would violate His Oneness and Unity. The metaphysical world, absolutely clear and transparent, contains none of the physical world's grossness. As Divine Power operates directly there, cause and effect have no effect, obstacles cannot interfere, and creating a particle is as easy as forming a sun.

To conclude, Divine Power is simple, infinite, and an indispensable Attribute of Divine "Essence." This Power operates directly in a realm that is clear, refined, and transparent, one in which there is nothing to oppose or intervene in it. Thus there is no difference between a community and an individual, particular and universal or big and small.

Third argument: Divine Power operates like a law that has the same relationship with everything. We shall make this subtle matter comprehensible through several comparisons or connections. Transparency, reciprocity, balance, orderliness, abstraction, and obedience are the phenomena in the universe that render many equal to few, and great equal to small.

First connection: Transparency. The same sun is reflected on the ocean's surface and a drop of water. If Earth consisted of pieces of glass, each one would reflect the sun without hindrance and without one interfering with the other. If the sun were a conscious independent being with willpower that could reflect its own light, its giving of light to or being reflected in one particle or on the whole Earth would be equally easy.

Second connection: Reciprocity. If we stand with a lit candle in the center of a large circle of people, each of whom is holding a mirror, each mirror will hold the same reflection without any one hindering any other.

Third connection: Balance. If we weigh a pair of things with a balance that measures each item with perfect precision, any extra force exerted upon either scale would disturb the balance.

Fourth connection: Orderliness. We can steer a huge ship as easily as a small toy, for all the parts of its orderly system are interrelated.

Fifth connection: Abstraction or Incorporeality. A living creature's size has no bearing on its real essence or nature, for these abstract and incorporeal features are the same for every creature. Differences in individualized forms do not cause confusion. For example, a minnow has the same essence or nature as a basking-shark (both are fish), and a micro-organism has the same essence as a rhinoceros (both are living animals).

Sixth connection: Obedience. A commander moves an army as easily as a single soldier by ordering it to march. The reality of obedience in the universe is as follows: Everything inclines toward its own perfection. An inclination grows into a need, an increased need becomes a yearning, and an increased yearning becomes an attraction. Inclination, need, yearning, and attraction work as Divine laws and operate in ways designed to lead things to realize their perfection. Creation's final, absolute perfection occurs when it grows into absolute existence. A thing's relative perfection is the relative existence that gives effect to all its potentialities. This is why the universe's obedience to the Divine Command of *"Be!" and it is* (36: 82) does not differ from that of a particle.

Creation obeys this Divine Command, coming from the Creator's Eternal Will, via the same forces of inclination, need, yearning, and attraction. All of these are urged to operate on all creatures by the same Divine Will. The power of this obedience is best seen in water, which cracks or even shatters iron when told to freeze.

Seeing that these defective, limited, weak, and non-creative contingent forces display such effects, everything is equally susceptible to the Divine Power's order. This Power is infinite, eternal, absolutely perfect, and can bring the universe into existence from non-existence. It also can manifest Itself through those grand works that fascinate and astound us. Nothing is difficult for it. Considering these six connections does not pass any judgment upon Divine Power, as it is impossible for us to do so; rather, they enable us to have some grasp of the matter.

In sum: Divine Power is infinite, an indispensable Attribute of the Supreme Being that operates in the metaphysical sphere, which has no obstacle or particularity. This domain is in direct contact with Divine Power, within which the material existence or non-existence of any thing is equally possible. It obeys all Divine laws of creation. Thus Divine Power can create everything with equal ease. For example, It can quicken creation on the Last Day as easily as It can revive an insect in spring. Given this, the Divine announcement of your creation and resurrection as a single soul is true and unexaggerated. This proves that the Agent Who will destroy and re-create the universe on the Last Day can do this.

FOURTH FUNDAMENTAL: As the Resurrection
is necessary, the One Who will raise the dead can
do this. The whole world is exposed to the
Resurrection. There are four related concepts here:
The world can perish, it will perish, the destroyed
world can be rebuilt as the Hereafter, and it will
be resurrected and rebuilt.

First matter: The death of creation is possible.
That which is subject to the law of development
must evolve to a final end. That which develops to
a final end must have a limited lifetime and, therefore, a fixed natural end. That which has a fixed end
inevitably dies. Humanity is a microcosm subject
to death; the universe can be regarded as a macro-
human being and therefore also subject to death.
Accordingly, it will perish and be resurrected on
the morning of the Last Day. Just as a living tree
(a miniature universe) cannot save itself from annihilation, the "branches of creatures" growing from
"the Tree of Creation" will pass away.

If the universe is not destroyed by an external
destructive event, with the Eternal Will's permission, it eventually will begin to die. Even scientists
say this. According to the Qur'an, it will give a
sharp cry, and then the following things will hap-

pen: *When the sun shall be darkened; when the stars shall be thrown down; when the mountains shall be set moving* (81:1-3) and *When heaven is split open; when the stars are scattered; when the seas swarm over* (82:1-3).

A significant subtle point: Water freezes and loses its essential liquid form, ice melts and loses its essential solid state, an item's essence becomes stronger at the expense of its material form, coarse language is not suitable for expressing meaning, the spirit weakens as the flesh becomes more substantial, and the flesh weakens as the spirit becomes more illuminated. Thus life gradually refines the solid world in favor of the afterlife. Creative Power breathes life into dense, solid, and inanimate substances as the result of astonishing activities, and refines that solid world to the advantage of the Hereafter through the light of life.

No truth, despite its weakness, ever perishes. Rather, it assumes a form in the corporeal world. As it flourishes and expands, its form grows weaker and more refined. The spiritual truth that constitutes an item's essence is inversely proportional to its form's strength. Thus the form grows denser as the truth weakens, and the truth becomes stronger as the form weakens. This law is common to whatever develops and evolves. Given this, the corporeal world, which is a form containing the great truth of the universe, will shatter, with the Majestic Creator's permission, and be rebuilt more beautifully. One day, *Upon the day Earth shall be changed to other than Earth* (14:48) will be realized, for the world can die.

Second matter: The world's eventual death is confirmed by all God-revealed religions, supported by all pure and saintly persons, and indicated by the universe's changes, transformations, and alterations. The constant replacement of this guesthouse's inhabitants, all of whom are welcomed and then leave at their appointed time (through death) so that they can be replaced by newcomers, also indicates this world's death.

Consider the Qur'anic description of the minute and precise interrelationship of the universe's constituent parts. Consider their sublime and delicate organization into a system. If any heavenly body were told to leave its axis, the universe would be thrown into the throes of death. Stars would collide, planets would be scattered, and the sound of exploding spheres would fill space. Mountains would begin to move, and Earth would be flattened. Eternal Power will bring about the next life in just this way, and the elements of Paradise and Hell will be separated from each other.

Third matter: The universe can be resurrected, for as proved in the Second Fundamental, Divine Power is not defective. Moreover, there is a strong necessity for it and it is possible. If there is a strong necessity that something possible should occur, it comes to be regarded as something that will occur.

Another significant point: A close examination of what occurs in the universe shows that it contains opposites that have spread everywhere and become rooted. The results of their clashes account for good and evil, benefit and harm, perfection and defect, light and darkness, guidance and misguidance, belief and unbelief, obedience and rebellion, and fear and love. Such ongoing conflict causes the universe to manifest a continuous alteration and transformation in order to produce the elements of a new world.

These opposed elements eventually will lead to eternity in two different directions and materialize as Paradise and Hell. The eternal world will be made up of this transitory world's essential elements, which will be given permanence. Paradise and Hell are the two opposite fruits growing on the Tree of Creation's two branches, the two results of the chain of creation, the two cisterns being filled by the two streams of things and events, the two poles to which beings flow in waves, and the places where Divine Grace and Divine Wrath manifest themselves. They will be filled with their particular inhabitants when Divine Power shakes up the universe.

This point is significant because God, the Eternal All-Wise and as the requirement of His Eternal Grace and Wisdom, has created this world as a testing arena, a mirror to reflect His Beautiful Names, a vast page upon which to write with the Pen of His Destiny and Power. People are tested here to develop their potentialities and to manifest their abilities. This emergence of abilities causes relative truths to appear in the universe, which, in turn, causes the Majestic Maker's Beautiful Names to manifest their inscriptions and make the universe a missive of the Eternally-Besought-of-All. In addition, this testing separates the diamond-like essences of sublime souls from the coal-like matter of base ones.

For His Own sublime purposes, God willed that creation, as well as its change and alteration, should take place. He made opposites confront one another—mingling harm with benefit, evil with good, and ugliness with beauty. Kneading them together like dough, He subjected the universe to the law of alteration and the principle of perfection. One day this testing and trial will end, and the Pen of Divine Destiny will have written what it has to write. Divine Power will have completed its work, all creatures will have fulfilled their duties and services, and seeds will have been sown in the field of the afterlife. The Earth will have displayed Divine Power's miracles, and this transitory world will have hung all eternal scenes upon the picture-rail of time.

The Majestic Maker's eternal Wisdom and Favor will require that the test's results be announced and that the truths of the Divine Beautiful Names' manifestations and the Pen of Divine Destiny's missives be unveiled. The duties performed by creatures will be repaid, the truths of the meanings expressed by the Book of the Universe's words will be seen, the fruits of potentialities will be yielded, a supreme court will be established, and the veil of natural causes will be removed so that everything is submitted directly to the Divine Will and Power.

On that day, the Majestic Creator will destroy the universe in order to eternalize it and separate its opposites. This separation will cause Hell to appear with all its awfulness, and Paradise to appear with all its beauty and splendor. The people of Hell will be threatened with: *Now keep yourselves apart, you sinners, upon this day* (36:59), while the People of Paradise will be welcomed with: *Peace be upon you. Well you have fared; enter in, to dwell forever* (39:73). By means of His perfect Power, the Eternal All-Wise will give an everlasting, unchanging existence to the inhabitants of both dwelling places. They will not age or suffer bodily disintegration or decomposition, for there will be nothing to cause any change.

Fourth matter: After destroying this world, the One Who created it will re-form it more beautifully and convert it into a mansion of the Hereafter. The Qur'an, which contains thousands of rational evidences, and other Divine Scriptures agree on this, as do the All-Majestic One's Attributes related to His Majesty, Grace, and Beautiful Names. Moreover, He promised that He would bring about the Resurrection and the Great Mustering through all of His heavenly decrees sent to His Prophets, all of whom agree that He carries out His promises. Prophet Muhammad is the foremost to confirm this, along with the strength of his 1,000 miracles. All saints and righteous scholars confirm this as well. Lastly, the universe predicts it with all the scientific evidence it contains.

In short, it is as certain as the sun's rising the next morning after setting this evening that the "sun of truth" will appear in the form of the Hereafter's life after this world's life sets.

Inspired by the Divine Name the All-Wise and the Qur'an's grace, I have elaborated the proofs of this truth to convince the intellect and ready the heart to accept it. But the words of the Creator of the universe have the greatest right to speak in this matter. So, listen to the Eternal Discourse of the All-Wise Maker, in which He addresses everyone regardless of time and place. In response, we must believe and affirm what He says:

When Earth is shaken with a mighty shaking and brings forth its burdens, and humanity asks: "What ails it?" Upon that day it shall give its tidings, for its Lord has inspired it. Upon that day people shall go forth in groups to receive requital for their former deeds, and whoever has done an atom's weight of good shall see it, and whoever has done an atom's weight of evil shall see it. (99:1-8)

Give good tidings to those who believe and do deeds of righteousness, that for them await gardens underneath which rivers flow. Whenever they are provided with fruits therefrom they shall say: "This is what we were provided with aforetime"; that they shall be given in perfect semblance; and that for them shall be spouses purified. They shall dwell therein forever. (2:25)

All glory be to You. We have no knowledge save what You have taught us. You are the All-Knowing, the All-Wise.

Our Lord, do not take us to task if we forget or make mistakes. O God, bestow blessings on our master Muhammad and on his Family, as You bestowed blessings on our master Abraham and his family. You are the All-Praiseworthy, All-Glorious.

Index